MORE SECRETS OF THE DEAD

MORE SECRETS
OF THE DEAD

HUGH MILLER

First published in 2001 by Channel 4 Books,
an imprint of Macmillan Publishers Ltd,
25 Eccleston Place, London SW1W 9NF,
Basingstoke and Oxford.

Associated companies throughout the world.

www.macmillan.com

ISBN 0 7522 1924 3

9 8 7 6 5 4 3 2 1

A CIP catalogue record for this book is available from the British Library.

Design and typesetting by Jane Coney
Colour reproduction by Aylesbury Studios
Printed and bound in Great Britain by Mackays of Chatham plc

CONTENTS

PRODUCTION CREDITS

THE JAMESTOWN MASSACRE
accompanies the *Secrets of the Dead* programme of the same name
made by Optomen Television for Channel 4.

BLOOD ON THE ALTAR
accompanies the *Secrets of the Dead* programme of the same name
made by Twenty Twenty Television for Channel 4.

MURDER AT STONEHENGE
accompanies the *Secrets of the Dead* programme of the same name
made by Yorkshire Associate Producers for Channel 4.

THE RIDDLE OF THE PLAGUE SURVIVORS
accompanies the *Secrets of the Dead* programme of the same name
made by Tigress Productions for Channel 4.

THE REAL ZULU DAWN
accompanies the *Secrets of the Dead* programme of the same name
made by Optomen Television for Channel 4.

1

THE JAMESTOWN MASSACRE

THERE IS A WIDESPREAD but mistaken belief that the history of modern America began with the arrival of 102 English exiles, the Pilgrim Fathers, at Plymouth in south-eastern Massachusetts in 1620. The story goes that these pious settlers, equipped with little more than faith, strong backs, and the determination to forge a new life for themselves, laid the foundation of America as we know it today.

The truth is not so romantic, and it is far less inspirational. The establishment of the first English settlement in America took place well south of Massachusetts, at Jamestown in Virginia. These settlers, 105 men and boys, arrived in Virginia nearly thirteen years before the Pilgrim Fathers set sail from England. They were gentlemen, artisans, and labourers, mainly from London and East Anglia. Their story, almost from the time they landed, is one of intense hardship and a daily struggle simply to stay alive. Within months of their arrival sixty-seven of their number had died, most of them in terrible pain. Over the following three years hundreds of others who came to swell the colony's numbers suffered the same miserable fate. Master George Percy, a member of the first colony, a councillor and brother of the Earl of Northumberland, wrote in his *Observations*, 'There were never Englishmen left in a foreign country in such misery as we were in this new discovered Virginia.'

Yet they had set out with the highest of expectations. On 10 April 1606, King James I issued a charter to the Virginia Company of London, granting them extensive colonization privileges. The charter stipulated that the territory lying between the 34th and 45th degrees of north latitude was available for settlement, plus the islands 'hereunto adjacent, or within one hundred miles of the coasts thereof'. A venture of territorial settlement would have been impossible without large-scale funding; the Virginia Company raised the money by issuing shares, and the issue was quickly bought up.

There were a number of sound reasons for the company wishing to establish a colony in America. Its members, being shareholders, expected a sound return on their investment, and colonization was considered a reliable first step in that direction. It was obvious that a port in Virginia, properly equipped and competently manned, would facilitate the wholesale import of English goods in exchange for commodities from the New World. It was predicted that vigorous trading would quickly be established, and every man in business knew that trading was the bedrock of growth and prosperity. Other stated reasons for establishing the colony included the setting up of an exploratory body to find a route to the East India Sea, or South Sea as it was then sometimes called, nowadays known as the Pacific Ocean. There was also the intention, noted in George Percy's *Observations*, to carry out a search for surviving descendants of Sir Walter Raleigh's ill-fated colony at Roanoke Island. The island, 12 miles long by 3 miles at its widest point, lies off the coast of North Carolina in what is now Dare County. After Raleigh had sent captains Arthur Barlowe and Philip Amadas to explore the territory in 1584, colonizing expeditions, which were the first made by the English into the New World, took place in 1585 and 1587. In 1587 the first child to be born to English parents in the New World arrived on 18 August: she was baptized Virginia Dare. Three years later the settlers had all vanished, and no evidence was found to explain what happened to them. In spite of promises given to the contrary, the administrators of the Virginia Company appear never to have organized an exploratory expedition; in fact it seems they never made any attempt to throw light on the mystery of Roanoke Island.

Inevitably, commercial imperatives had a powerful influence on the planning of the colonization at Virginia. One serious and urgent aim was to establish a foothold in North America in order to halt, or at least hamper, the further colonial spread of Spain in the same area. It was also a priority to find as many commodities and crops as possible, particularly any that the English were currently obliged to buy from Europe at extortionate prices. Colonists were briefed to seek out reliable sources of furs, cordage, masts, planks, pitch, tar, potash, hemp, flax, iron, grapes and other fruits, salt, silk, roots and berries, medicinal plants and herbs, oils and gums, cotton, silk grass (for rope-making), sugar cane, and grains.

In the terms of the charter the King emphasized that the colonists must spread the Christian faith 'to such people as yet live in darkness and miserable ignorance of the true knowledge and worship of God'. At the same time his majesty had his own pecuniary agenda, and in the text of a letter of incentive to the prospective colonists he exhorted them to find mineral wealth, 'Dig, delve and hew for all manner of deposits and residues of gold, silver, and copper...'

The settlers, on the face of it, had reason enough to set out in good heart. Even the ones who were from the yeoman class, men with no shares in the Virginia Company, were drawn to join the venture for a chance to better themselves. In the seventeenth century that usually meant finding a piece of land to farm, and Virginia seemed to offer every opportunity for that kind of initiative. Few forays into the New World had been more vigorously motivated, more smiled-upon by monarchy, or better funded. Yet the dream soon curdled to nightmare.

Over the years historians and scientific investigators have put forward a number of explanations for the calamities of the early years of the Jamestown settlement, but there has never been general agreement on precisely where the blame should be laid. There is evidence to back the view that the colonists brought their troubles on their own heads, largely because of their rancour, their frequent disagreements, and their consequent failure to adopt long-term policies for survival and expansion. Whatever the root cause of their failure to thrive, the most commonly held theory about how so many of them died is that they starved for want of adequate supplies of food. Records made by survivors certainly tell of famine on a pitiful scale, but they also describe harrowing levels of infection and illness, and several present-day investigators believe that disease was the principal cause of death among the early English settlers.

The original Jamestown site was a peninsula on the James River in Virginia. The colony fell into decay after the Virginian seat of government was moved, in 1699, to the Middle Plantation, later called Williamsburg. For many years the colony was believed to have been lost forever, but in the mid-nineteenth century, by which time erosion had caused the peninsula to become an island, vigorous action by conservationists arrested the general decay at the site, and archaeological excavations uncovered traces of the original fort. Specialist study at the site continues to this day and their work, notably that of Dr Bill Kelso and his team on the Jamestown Rediscovery Project, has produced an abundance of artefacts that have begun to recreate, vividly, the structure and day-to-day life of the colony.

Another avenue of research, independent of the work of Kelso and his colleagues, has produced a controversial theory which suggests that the truth behind the deaths of so many colonists is a good deal more sinister than anyone had previously suspected. 'The study of the early colony of Jamestown is very intriguing,' said Dr Frank Hancock, a pathologist with a special interest in early colonial history. 'I think the gentlemen who came, and those who came with them, were appropriately chosen. I think the plan instituted by the Virginia Company was appropriate and it should have succeeded. The disaster that befell the colony I think occurred because of two separate or perhaps interrelated instances. One can see significant political disruption in the leadership, and one can also see significant physical disruption in what may well have been sabotage.'

The sabotage referred to by Dr Hancock was, specifically, poisoning. To gain a perspective on his startling theory, it is best to view this seventeenth-century enigma from its beginning, and to take account of suppositions that have accumulated from separate areas of research into the Jamestown phenomenon.

The 105 men chosen to settle the territory set sail from Blackwall on the Thames on 20 December 1606. A ship's log records that one of them, Edward Brookes, died of heat exhaustion and thirst on the island of Mona in the West Indies on 7 April 1607, less than three weeks before they reached their destination. They travelled in three ships, the *Susan Constant*, the *Godspeed*, and the *Discovery*, under the overall command of Captain Christopher Newport. It was a voyage which should have taken weeks, but ended up taking much longer. 'By unprosperous winds,' wrote George Percy, '[we] were kept six weeks in the sight of England.' The diary of another of the settlers, Captain John Smith, records, 'We were at sea five months, where we spent our vittle and lost the time and season to plant.'

On such a long, tedious, cramped journey it was inevitable that disputes would break out, and the strain of political tension couldn't have helped. Among many uncertainties, there was the matter of who would be in charge of the colony. 'On the way over they carried sealed orders which weren't to be opened until they got there,' said Ivor Noël Hume, an archaeologist and the author of *The Virginia Adventure*. 'So the CEO hadn't been advertised and all these gentlemen were jockeying for that position. There must have been a tremendous sense of tension throughout the entire voyage. So much so that John Smith, who always spoke when he wasn't expected to, wound up in irons.'

They finally landed at Cape Henry, at the mouth of the James River where it enters Chesapeake Bay, on 26 April 1607. As soon as they were anchored the seal on the box of orders was broken. 'That night was the box opened,' recorded settler Thomas Studley, 'and the orders read: in which Bartholomew Gosnoll, Edward Wingfield, Christopher Newport, John Smith, John Ratcliffe, John Martin, and George Kendall, were named to be the Council, and to choose a President amongst them for a year, who with the Council should govern. Matters of moment were to be examined by a Jury, but determined by the major part of the Council in which the President had two voices.'

John Smith, being so sharply elevated in the community, was promptly released from irons.

The two weeks immediately following the landing at Cape Henry were spent exploring the James River for a suitable place to establish a settlement. On 14 May they finally decided on a peninsula 50 miles from the mainland coast. It was a decision reached only after bitter argument. Discord aside, however, the settlers were fundamentally buoyant and full of expectation. They and the governors and shareholders of the London Virginia Company were flushed with the excitement of prospectors approaching territory as yet unplundered. The moment of commencement had arrived. George Percy described their first day in the settlement. 'The fourteenth day, we landed all our men; which were set to work about the fortification, and others, some to watch and ward, as it was convenient.

'The first night of our landing, about midnight, there came some Savages sailing close to our quarter. Presently there was an alarum given; upon that, the Savages ran away, and we [were] not troubled any more by them that night.'

Captain John Smith also recorded the events of that momentous day. 'Arriving at the place where we are now seated, the Council was sworn, and the President elected, which for that year was Master Edm. Maria Wingfield, where was made choice for our situation, a very fit place for the erecting of a great city, about which some contention passed betwixt Captain Wingfield and Captain Gosnold: notwithstanding, all our provision was brought ashore, and with as much speed as might be, we went about our fortification.'

Beverly Straube, curator of the Jamestown Rediscovery Project, explained the urgency behind the raising of fortifications. 'When the colonists came, the main concern was that the Spanish would attack them and try to drive them out, because they would see the English as a threat to their settlements further south. That threat never materialized, but on the other hand the type of fortifications that the English built served basically as protection against the Native Americans. They wouldn't have withstood a full-fledged military attack. They were wary on all fronts, but the real concern was about an attack by the Spanish.'

Anxieties about defences, however, were soon taking second place to serious disappointment. 'Right from the start they were thinking of gold and silver as being the principal return,' said Ivor Noël Hume. 'What they found was there wasn't any gold. Nor was there any silver. But there was wood, a lot of wood, and there was pitch and tar. And so they started to ship that back, and this is, I think, one of the things that probably upset the artisans and labourers because they really had expected they were going to have little nuggets to put in their pouches, you know? And all they got after all was hard work.'

That hot Virginian summer the settlers' major priority remained the fortification of the settlement against the old Spanish enemy. In the scrambling lust for empire each side knew that the other was prepared to commit slaughter either in pursuit of expansion or to protect their existing territory.

The imminent danger to the settlers, however, lay nearer at hand. The region was populated by dozens of Native American tribes, amalgamated for strength under the leadership of the powerful chief Powhatan. He was the son of an Algonquin chief whose tribe migrated south to Virginia during the sixteenth century. Powhatan's father had fought and conquered five of the resident Virginian tribes and set up a confederacy of six tribes. When Powhatan succeeded his father, he drew a further twenty-four tribes into the confederacy. Though a spectacularly cruel man, Powhatan was a clever and conscientious leader. He was also the father of Pocahontas, who famously interceded, at the age of thirteen, to save Captain John Smith's life at the hands of her father's warriors – or so Captain Smith would one day claim.

Within days of the settlers' arrival, and long before their fortifications were even close to being adequate, they were attacked by one of Powhatan's war parties. There is no record of anyone being killed, but a number of men were wounded and after several subsequent attacks it became clear that Powhatan's warriors far outnumbered the settlers, who could easily have been routed or even massacred if Powhatan had chosen. Hostilities somehow had to be suspended, at least until the settlers were better protected. Eventually a fragile truce was established, due in part to the bestowing of gifts to the Native Americans, and in part to the diplomacy of John Smith.

The three ships that brought the settlers to Virginia left for the return journey to England in June 1607. They were scarcely out of sight when colonists began falling ill and dying. John Smith was one of the very few original settlers who survived to record the events of that dark time. 'Being thus left to our fortunes,' he wrote, 'it fortuned that within ten days scarce ten amongst us could either go or stand, such extreme weakness and sickness oppressed us.'

The affliction was as severe as its onset was swift, and it quickly depleted the settlement. Within eight months the population of 104 had shrunk to thirty-eight. Of the 500 additional people who came to Jamestown from England between 1607 and 1610, fewer than sixty survived. The cause of such a staggering mortality rate – over 80 per cent – remains one of the great mysteries of early colonial life in America.

Now, nearly 400 years later, the Jamestown story has dwindled to a few short entries in the popular history books. Commentators believe that its loss of stature as a significant milestone in world history is mirrored by the physical decline of the settlement itself. Over the years the neglected fort site simply crumbled and drifted away on the river, apparently taking with it, piece by piece, every last clue to what had happened there. That was the information given to Dr Bill Kelso when he visited the island as a student in the late 1960s. 'I felt that I would be able to see the place where everything started,' he said, 'and I asked a park ranger where was the fort, and he pointed to the river and said "Somewhere out there". And I was crushed, you know. I'd come all this way...'

After his initial shock, and following a careful reconnaissance of the island, Kelso began to suspect that early excavators at Jamestown had simply not recognized the remains of the fort. They had missed the signs, or they had failed to interpret them correctly. It was thirty years later, with a distinguished career in archaeology to give weight to his conjecture, that Kelso was finally allowed to prove he was right. 'It was a staff of one,' he said. 'I mean it was just me at the time, and when the shovel went in the ground it was fingers crossed. Fortunately I found artefacts right away, and they were from the right period. And I was elated. I walked over to a seat on the edge of the river and just sat down and just smiled, big time. Wow! This was gonna be a real adventure.'

That low-key, one-man beginning has grown to become the Jamestown Rediscovery Project, of which Kelso is Director of Archaeology. It is a major long-term excavation which has so far produced hundreds of thousands of artefacts from the settlement period. For a long time, however, no traces were found of the settlers themselves. Then one day in 1996 the team uncovered the skeleton of a young man. It was given the uninspiring name of JR102C. As centuries of accumulated dirt and debris were carefully brushed away from the bones, a musket ball was discovered lodged in the skeleton's right leg, a few inches below the knee. That was why they tacked the initials 'JR' to the skeleton, Kelso explained: it appeared the young settler had died from a massive gunshot wound. 'I think that there was a major civil unrest situation going on, especially after people started dying like flies. Mostly it was a mutiny. There were a lot of different factions that either wanted to leave or wanted to change the leadership.'

Kelso conducted ballistic tests, using replica muskets to try and find out what had possibly happened. Could JR, for instance, have accidentally shot himself? 'We tested all the various types of weapons that could have been used at the time on targets, to see how far back we needed to go to get a spread of shot that would reflect the spread of shot in the wound. And it had to be at least eight feet away. JR did *not* shoot himself.'

Various foul-play scenarios suggested themselves, all prompted by the same question: who shot JR? But if the answer was to provide genuine enlightenment about the first terrible years at Jamestown, it would have to be established that JR had actually been one of the settlers, not a Native American, and not the remains of a much later burial. Pieces of ceramic pots and fragments of ornaments found mixed in the soil close to the skeleton suggested that JR really was from the early settlement period, but by themselves these were an inadequate basis for a conclusion. If JR had been one of the early settlers then he would have grown up in England. The proof or disproof of his English origin would be preserved in the one part of the body that doesn't change even after centuries in the ground. The enamel of the teeth acts as an organic archive of an individual's life, creating a detailed history which is readable to those who know how to translate the signs. One such person is Dr Paul Budd at Bradford University in Yorkshire. Kelso sent him one of JR's teeth. 'The reason we look at a tooth,' said Budd, 'is because the tooth enamel preserves material that a person has consumed, or elements from the person's diet during life. Some of those elements can tell us something about where the person actually came from – where he or she actually grew up. Enamel is formed in early childhood, unlike various other tissues in the body like bone, which is remodelled and changes over a lifetime. With enamel, once it's formed that's it, it's fixed. It's not going to change again.'

In the laboratory a high-intensity laser beam was directed at a powdered sample of JR's tooth enamel, causing it to vaporize. The vaporization, in its turn, released certain atoms of oxygen which would identify elements of the water JR drank as his enamel was going through its formative phase. The atoms were collected in the form of vapour so that their aggregated data could be examined in a mass spectrometer. Mass spectrometry identifies materials by isolating their atoms in a gas and then counting them, using magnetic and electrical fields to perform the separation. Specific numbers of *specific* atoms pinpoint the nature of a substance within the sample. It is an advanced, sophisticated detection technique, and in the case of JR it was being used to extract data relating to the presence of the element strontium in his tooth enamel. This would indicate the geology of the area where JR was raised. The procedure was complex and time consuming, but the result was not at all ambiguous. The spectrometry pinpointed Cornwall as the area where JR was most likely to have grown up.

So the deceased had been an Englishman and therefore almost certainly one of the early Jamestown settlers. With that much established, what useful evidence could his remains provide about his time at the settlement? To find out, Kelso sent the bones to be analyzed by one of the world's leading forensic anthropologists, Dr Doug Owsley, at the Smithsonian Institution in Washington DC. 'There's nothing in the archeological record you can recover that can tell you more about a past people than the opportunity to learn from the bones themselves,' said Owsley. 'A skeleton can tell you volumes and in the case of JR he's a very special fellow. He's full of mystery. We've been trying to figure him out for more than two years and we still have lots of things that we don't understand.'

The first data Owsley established were JR's sex and age. 'There's no question in my mind that this is a male,' he said, holding up various bones as he spoke. 'The features that I see in the pelvis, in the size and length of the long bones, the definition of the muscle attachment areas at different locations, those are all male characteristics. In the same sense when you're talking about a male skull, males tend to have more slope to the forehead on average, whereas females tend to have a much more vertical forehead. Those features all identify this individual as a male.

'With regard to age, one of the things that we look at in this individual is his tibia, his shinbone. The proximal tibia still has a well-defined growth-plate line, indicating that this individual was still growing. And again, comparing it to known reference samples, you can use that to assign an age to an individual.'

A reconstruction was made of JR's head, using a replica of the skull as the template. Broad muscle groups fashioned from clay were distributed over the skull at positions and in proportions typical of a male of JR's race, age, and stature. This process was refined until a simulation of all the smooth underlying muscle and adjacent tissues of the human head and face had been created.

The painstaking work carried out at this stage conformed to standard, tabulated soft-tissue measurements, making sure that the bulk and contour of the reproduction was consistent with established standards and norms. Simulated skin and hair were added to the head, then the recreation was finished with artificial eyes. The result was a startlingly lifelike replica of the head of a normal, healthy looking young man, approximately twenty years old.

Both the identity of JR and the person who killed him remain the subject of investigation. But one thing is clear: JR was a gentleman. Gentlemen who died were buried in coffins and within the confines of the fort. Those who were not classified as gentlemen, in other words the rank and file, were wrapped in shrouds and buried in shallow graves in the woods. Another reasonable certainty is that the shooting of JR was deliberate. Bill Kelso points out that muskets, in addition to being complicated and difficult to load and fire, do not easily go off by accident. Kelso talked of the shock of discovering JR's wound. 'We went down the leg, and then suddenly here was this musket ball in the bone. At that moment I understood something about how traumatic or how challenging it was to be at Jamestown, because if a person was shot we would expect to find arrow points. I said "Wait, you know what this means? A European weapon killed this guy. It's unlikely the Indians had that kind of weapon, if this dates to that 1607 period.' Kelso found it easy to picture what had been going on. 'They were shooting each other. Either accidentally or on purpose. There was also unrest, sure, and if you think about it, well... when people are starving, the rules change.'

On examining JR's injured leg, Bill Owsley discovered that fragments of lead were scattered throughout several centimetres of bone around the spot where the musket ball had lodged. He also noted that a cut had been made in the ball, which would have caused it to fragment, at least partially, on impact with its target. It had been a deeply unpleasant way to die, and another settler had almost certainly fired the gun. Even so, as intriguing as the mystery of JR's death undoubtedly is, it cannot stand as an indicator of what went so disastrously wrong at Jamestown. Infighting certainly occurred, it is clearly chronicled, but JR's skeleton is the only one recovered so far that shows signs of death by shooting.

The latest archaeological findings support the traditionally held view that the settlers were brought down by the twin scourges of disease and starvation. So extreme was their hunger that they turned to cannibalism. George Percy provides a stark chronicle of the winter of 1609, known in local folklore as the 'Starving Time'. 'We were driven through unsufferable hunger unnaturally to eat those things which nature most abhorred, the flesh and excrement of man. And one of our own nation tells of an Indian digged by some out of his grave after he had lain buried three days and wholly devoured him. One amongst the rest did kill his wife, salted her, and had eaten half of her before it were known, for which he was executed, as he well deserved.'

At the site of the Jamestown fort strong evidence has emerged to suggest that most of the settlers simply starved to death. Bill Kelso described a cellar recently unearthed by the Rediscovery team. 'It was probably here in 1610, Captain John Smith could have even walked in here. When it was abandoned it was filled in with over thirty thousand artefacts that had been thrown away as just trash. We found a lot of bones of animals that could have been eaten. So it's probably material that was here from a traumatic time like the Starving Time years of 1609 and 1610.'

George Percy's account tells of the variety of animals that had to serve as food. 'Famine compelled us wholly to devour those hogs, dogs and horses that were then in the colony, together with rats, mice, snakes, or what vermin or carrion so ever we could light on.'

Beverly Straube found that physical evidence from the cellar corroborated the surviving chronicles of the time. 'They tell us how they cut their horses up into dainty squares and ate them,' she said. 'They'd never have eaten their horses at home. We have elements of horse legs and you can actually see the chop marks along the edges where the horse has definitely been butchered. And they do tell us that they had to eat the rats as well, and the evidence is here. This is the first appearance of black rats in the New World. We're seeing rapidly here what they're telling us in the records, that they had to resort to eating things that they normally wouldn't.'

Until now it has never been entirely clear why food was in such short supply. During a routine climate survey Dennis Planton, an archaeologist, made a discovery that may provide an answer. 'It's hard to imagine how anyone could have starved at Jamestown,' he said. 'The site is surrounded by a very rich natural area. The streams are full of fish, crabs, oysters, and the forests are full of food of various kinds.'

It had always been the plan that the settlers would trade for food with the Native Americans and thereby eliminate the need to grow it on any scale or hunt for it themselves. The plan went badly wrong, however, when the natives insisted they had no food to spare. And Dennis Planton, using dendrochronology, discovered why. Dendrochronology is the science of arranging events in their proper time order by studying characteristics of growth rings in ancient timber. Planton extracted the relevant facts from the old trees around Jamestown. 'We're fortunate to have some of the earliest trees in the country there,' he said. 'There are some that are over a thousand years old and there are enough of them, potentially, to allow us to reconstruct the climate. There's one type that consistently lives to that age at Jamestown – it's the bald cypress tree. It grows in wet environments, but we also know it's very sensitive to wet and dry conditions.'

Planton obtained his tree samples using an increment borer, a metal tube with a small enough bore to ensure it will do the tree no harm. The borer is screwed into the trunk of a tree to extract a core sample which extends from the bark of the tree to its centre. In the laboratory, the rings are counted and measured, then the ring sequence is compared to sequences from standardized core samples. The success of the procedure relies on the fact that many species of trees produce growth rings during their annual growing seasons. Various factors determine the amount of annual growth, but it tends to fluctuate in proportion either to the amount of available rain or the prevailing temperatures. The precise measurement of rings made from trees with overlapping ages can provide climate information from thousands of years ago.

Planton's suspicion was that there had been a drought at the time the settlers arrived in Virginia. To find out if that was the case, he sent his delicate core samples to the University of Arkansas for specialized analysis. 'No one had ever implicated drought in the studies before,' Planton said, 'so my notion was received with a bit of scepticism both at Jamestown and in Arkansas. But lo and behold, they discovered from these tree rings that the worst drought in the last seven hundred and seventy years occurred between the years 1606 and 1612.'

So it was now clear that the English settlers had suffered their Starving Time four years into a severe drought. They had established a system whereby they would trade for corn with the Native Americans, but it can be assumed the drought produced such poor harvests that the Indians could scarcely feed themselves, let alone supply the colony. Yet however believable mass starvation may seem, both as it was recorded and from the evidence of archeological discoveries, there are accounts which contradict the starvation scenario and tell of an abundant supply of food, even during the so-called Starving Time. This anomaly has not been lost on Dr Frank Hancock, pathologist and keen student of Virginian history. 'While this starvation was going on in Jamestown,' he said, 'down at Point Comfort Captain James Davies was living quite well, and the record states that they had sufficient food to be able to feed the excess to their hogs. So we have hogs about forty miles or thereabouts downriver, we have excess food to feed those hogs, and yet at Jamestown they're starving. This doesn't seem to fit well.'

Point Comfort would have been easy to reach with the colonists' boat at Jamestown. It is highly probable they would have known about the abundant food there, yet they didn't go and take any for themselves. On the other hand, if they were suffering the awful afflictions described in the chronicles, they may simply have been too sick and feeble to set sail.

An influential thesis entitled *Environment, Disease, and Mortality in Early Virginia*, published in the 1970s by the human geographer Carville Earle, proposed that the main cause of death at Jamestown was not starvation at all, but disease. Earle believed that the water of the James River carried a fatal contamination, and that the colonists were obliged to drink it because there was no supply of fresh water at Jamestown. In the light of Earle's theory, the decision to make their settlement in a low-lying marshy location had been a lethal error of judgement.

Ivor Noël Hume, author of *The Virginia Adventure*, agrees that the choice of location might have been ill judged, but he can see the settlers' reasoning. 'People have always said what a stupid place to put a settlement, and if you're talking in terms of health, the higher ground would have been a great deal better. But from a strategic point of view it wasn't too bad. The ships could moor close to shore. That means that help could come ashore very easily, and if you had to, you could get out very easily. And you really can't fault them for not worrying about health when they first arrived. You don't worry about health until you find you aren't healthy.'

The chronicle of George Percy confirms that without fresh spring water on Jamestown Island the settlers had to drink water from the river, which was frequently foul and could even be deadly: 'Our drink was cold water taken out of the river which was full of slime and filth which was the destruction of many of our men'.

Carville Earle has advanced the view that the slimy filth was caused by the settlers' own sewage which, because of its volume, its density, the frequency of its production and the nature of the river currents, could only ever be partially washed away from the vicinity of the settlement. The problems arising from such a source of contagion would have been far worse during the drier months of summer. 'We speculated that waste entering the river from the area of the fort really didn't travel very far,' said Dennis Planton. 'It circulated with the tide, back and forth. The settlers were drinking that water, which at some stage would have become diseased, and that would have exacerbated many of the health problems they already faced.'

Dr Frank Hancock takes issue with the reports of poor quality water and with the suggestion of a certain feckless inability on the part of the settlers to look after themselves. 'The water in Jamestown during my visits in the twentieth century always seemed pleasant to me,' he said, 'and I could not understand why the colonists' water was reported to be of such poor quality. There is a tidal basin on the back side of Jamestown Island and the water would appear to be somewhat brackish in that area. But out front, where they most likely got their water, is the broad, deep, ever-flowing James River which would appear at least in the early 1600s to have been a very good source of water. The issue of sanitary habits also struck me as unusual in that most of the men who came here were gentlemen who'd had military training, and their leaders had had military training. In what little time I spent in the military I was trained to have good sanitary habits, especially on an expeditionary type of mission. So I found it somewhat odd to read that the water was of poor quality, and that these gentlemen did not know how to survive in the wilderness. It did not strike me as an appropriate consideration, and from those two reasons, basically, I began to have some doubts regarding the explanations for their deaths.'

Whatever the truth of the quality of water, or of the general competence of the settlers, their journals give copious descriptions of the diseases that assailed them. George Percy reports, 'The 6th day of August there died John Ashby of the bloody flux. Our people are indeed strangely afflicted with fluxes, agues.' Elsewhere he notes, 'Our men were destroyed with cruel diseases such as fluxes and burning fevers.'

In old medical terminology a flux was the name given to an excessive outpouring of blood, excrement, or any other matter from the bowels or other organs; the terms 'red flux', 'flux of blood' and 'bloody flux' were all early names for dysentery. As for the burning fevers, Carville Earle identified them as typhus. His arguments for water-borne disease being the main cause of the deaths at Jamestown are persuasive, but some points are open to dispute. For example, the settlers would have been well aware of the dangers of drinking contaminated water, but even if they had gone ahead and drunk it, would its effects really have been so devastating? 'I often wonder about this, because the Thames in London at this time was polluted,' said Ivor Noël Hume. 'The Walbrook stream which came down through Moorfields was clogged with rubbish and yet people were drinking out of it. I'm not sure the water at Jamestown was any worse. In fact it was possibly a little better than some of the water that people were drinking in London at that time.'

Earle's ideas on the dangers of river water mainly concern the summer months, when he believed the James River would have been most polluted. Yet the worst time for the English at Jamestown, the time when their death rate reached its zenith, was in the winter.

The exceptionally high mortality is not fully explained by any of the long-standing theories. Internal disagreements and squabbles amongst the colonists did not kill large numbers of them, if indeed they were the cause of any deaths at all. Starvation on the other hand does seem to have killed many of the settlers, though perhaps, as has already been suggested, that was because they were too weak to fetch the food that appears to have been available. This physical weakness is often mentioned in the surviving records, so from the weight of reference it would appear to have been a distinct reality. It could have been the result of disease or, as Dr Frank Hancock believes, it may have been something far more disquieting. He is convinced that his proposal offers the solution to so much that is ambiguous and unexplained about the death toll at Jamestown. There is no suggestion in his proposal that the settlers died of any natural cause. He believes they were murdered. It does appear that many of the settlers died displaying symptoms that were not typical of the diseases suggested in the traditional theories. George Percy and Captain John Smith both reported unusual manifestations. 'Master Scrivener lay exceedingly sick of a mad fever…' 'On the ninth day died George Flower of a swelling…' 'The tenth day died William Tarvener, bruised and swollen…' 'Sam Collier died suddenly…'

Reports show that amongst the dead and dying there were severe abdominal swellings, peeling skin, extreme lassitude, episodes of apparent madness, mysteriously sudden deaths – a catalogue, in fact, of symptoms and cessations that bore no signs typical of typhus, dysentery, or starvation. 'Some have licked up the blood which has fallen from their fellows.' 'Hugh Price, being pinched with extreme famine, in a furious distracted mood did come openly into the market place, blaspheming, exclaiming and crying out that there was no God.'

The notion of there being just one underlying cause of all those bizarre and lethal symptoms, a single source of such a gaggle of miseries, is intriguing, and it is the line of thought Dr Hancock pursued. He considered the records hard and long, he trawled his own considerable experience and learning, and finally he closed in on a one-culprit explanation for all the strange symptoms at Jamestown. The answer, he believed, was poisoning, and the poison in question was arsenic.

Hancock is Medical Director of one of the largest pathology laboratories in the world, and a member of one of Virginia's oldest families. He has always been fascinated by the Jamestown settlement and its shadowy history, but as a pathologist he was never persuaded by the complicated reasons given for the extinction of so many settlers. The scale of fatalities was epidemic, and Hancock knew very well that in the study of fatal epidemics it is customary to look for a sole cause. 'As I searched back through my memory of some years of medical practice,' he said, 'I began to consider a poisoning episode. I began to think of what would be the common poisons at the time, and arsenic poisoning became a concept that seemed rational to me.'

Hancock's suspicions were first raised by the sudden onset of the settlers' debilitating symptoms. 'Everything seemed fine until the time the original ships left to go back to England. Then John Smith says that within approximately ten days hardly anyone could stand or walk. This seems a rather sudden change.'

To put it another way, this abrupt change seemed to happen when it became impossible for the settlers to raise an alarm or to escape, should the need have arisen. The deaths happened in distinctly episodic outbreaks, which suggested to Hancock the hand of man rather than the intervention of disease or starvation. Tantalizing light began to dawn on the mystery as Hancock pursued his investigation with clinical rigour. His main priority at that stage was to arrive at a plausible diagnosis of the settlers' illness, based on the symptoms described in the old records. 'These people are no longer alive, obviously,' he said, 'so they cannot be interviewed. All that I had were the writings of George Percy and John Smith. So I went back and read these again, and I just jotted down any adjective, any phrase, anything that might be construed as a clinical sign or symptom.'

He found that while typhus and dysentery could account for a few of the symptoms, poisoning by arsenic could explain them all. Arsenic can cause the explosive, bloody diarrhoea and the burning fevers suffered by many dying settlers, symptoms which have hitherto been attributed to dysentery and typhus. Hancock also found that delusions and apparently psychotic behaviour on the part of some settlers appear among the documented effects of poisoning by arsenic. It can cause other symptoms mentioned in the records: swellings, a famished appearance, weakness so extreme it could believably have prevented victims from making the effort to find food. It is notable in this connection that a feature of arsenic poisoning, at certain levels, is paralysis of the muscles of the wrists and ankles, which would certainly have inhibited movement. It is significant, also, that while Percy's and Smith's accounts of bruising and sudden deaths were not consistent with a diagnosis of either typhus or dysentery, they are certainly typical of arsenic poisoning.

Coincidence caused Hancock to make another significant connection. It happened when the features of a case of murder in his home town paralleled details in the accounts of the suffering at Jamestown. The murder victim, a local man whose girlfriend had poisoned him with arsenic, had suffered chronic peeling of the skin for some time prior to his death. Hancock remembered from the records that some of the settlers had suffered the same thing, the skin in some cases coming off from head to foot. Hancock said, 'The skin exfoliation episode occurred when a group of settlers were sent to what was known as the Oyster Banks to live, because the food supply there was plentiful. They described an episode of their skins peeling off, so I searched one of my general textbooks and discovered that exfoliative dermatitis was mentioned as one of the possible consequences of arsenic poisoning.'

Poisonings and poisoning plots were common in early seventeenth-century Europe. Because arsenic in solution is colourless and practically without odour, it was the poison of choice at court and in the more homicidal aristocratic circles. 'It's my understanding,' said Hancock, 'that there were two commercial uses of arsenic. One use was by women who would carry it so that they could take a small taste from time to time in order to induce paleness, because paleness was desirable at that time.' The second common commercial use was as a poison for vermin, and there is evidence that it existed at Jamestown in this form. John Smith mentions a poison known as ratsbane which was used by the settlers to control vermin. It would certainly have been freely available aboard ship on the crossing to Virginia. The *Oxford English Dictionary* defines ratsbane as arsenic.

As Hancock grew to believe firmly that poisoning was the answer to the riddle, the shocking proposition that a poisoner could have been at work seemed ever more likely. Could Jamestown have harboured a traitor, or an agent from England's principal enemy, Spain? The suggestion flies in the face of accepted history. 'The theory that there was a conspiracy,' said Bill Kelso, 'someone purposely poisoning people at Jamestown, to me... well, it *is* possible, but it's not probable. I don't see enough evidence that says that's the case. There were plenty of ways to die there besides that. I mean there was just *everything* else.'

Ivor Noël Hume, on the other hand, didn't find the poisoning theory too extraordinary, especially when viewed in the light of other events. 'You think that's probably a dumb suggestion, but then of course the CIA and MI5 have done some pretty crazy things too. But in actual fact it could have happened, it really could, because following a massacre by the Chesapeake tribe in 1622, when the English went up to have a peace conference with their chief, the physician for Jamestown, Dr Potter, brewed up poisoned ale and they took it with them, and as a result they poisoned two hundred Indians including the chief and all his family and all his lords and so on. Having done that, they then slaughtered another fifty and came back to Jamestown saying "Wow! That was great, God was on our side!" They really said that, you know. So it could have happened.'

At the time of the Jamestown deaths a diagnosis of arsenic poisoning would have been difficult to make, and even its symptoms would not have been particularly easy to identify. Nowadays, of course, biochemists and toxicologists can detect the presence of arsenic in a body very quickly, and its mode of action is well understood. It is one of a group of elements known as heavy metals, so named because of their high specific gravity, and the human body readily absorbs it. It is stored in the liver and from there it passes into the general circulation. It is slowly eliminated from the system in the urine, the faeces, and in sweat. Although the intestines can eliminate a certain amount of arsenic from the body, the kidneys are the organs most vigorously involved in excreting the poison. When a single dose of arsenic is taken, it can be found in the urine in less than an hour; and it will continue to show up in the urine for ten or fourteen days or even longer. Following several doses, the kidneys, bowels, and sweat glands may continue excreting arsenic for up to three months. Absorbed arsenic is found in greatest quantity in the liver, and in the course of a few days it produces fatty changes in the liver's structure. In two or three weeks following recovery from a single dose, all traces of arsenic may have left the bodily systems, but signs will still be found in the hair, nails, skin, and bones. Arsenic will not normally be found in the hair until about a week after it has been taken, but it can go on being eliminated into the hair for long periods, and its presence there will persist even after all traces have left the organs. The amount of the poison found in different parts of the intestines is highly important in fatal cases, because it shows roughly how much time elapsed between administration of the drug and the death of the victim. Arsenic found in the upper part of the small intestine indicates that the interval would be between three and six hours. It would take about ten hours for it to reach the lower part of the small intestine, and roughly twelve hours to appear in the large intestine.

So the scientific procedures for detecting arsenic are well established, but if the detection is ever to take place at all, samples of soft tissue, hair, or nails of the suspected victim are required. All such remains are long gone from Jamestown. Nevertheless, in an effort to be as thorough and as painstaking as he could, Dr Hancock obtained a quantity of precious human bone from Jamestown and asked a colleague, toxicologist Richard Early, to carry out a sophisticated test capable of revealing infinitesimal traces of the poison. While it was extremely unlikely that there would be any arsenic in the bone after 400 years, the test was nevertheless an avenue which could be pursued, and since it was probably the only one, Hancock took it.

The sample was analyzed using a plasma mass spectrometer, which identifies and separates ions (atoms which have gained an electrical charge) according to the ratio between their mass and their charge. The equipment, working in conjunction with a computer, can detect the tiniest traces of elements and compounds in a given sample. In the case of the Jamestown bone it recorded the presence of heavy metals, including arsenic. 'In essence what we came up with,' explained Richard Early, 'was a small presence of these metals. The level was down in the lower parts-per-million range.'

Compelling as the results were, they were inconclusive, because with traces at those levels the bone could simply have been contaminated by naturally occurring elements from the surrounding soil. Nevertheless, Hancock was satisfied that he now had clinical proof of the reason for the settlers' deaths. Having found the means, he was faced with the task of determining a motive. And what about the malefactor himself? Who could that have been? 'I set aside the medical issues,' said Hancock. 'I went back to reading general history, which took me back to England, where I had to consider internal English politics and see how the divisions within England were interacting with Spain.'

The main political struggle in England at the time was still between Protestant and Catholic factions. Only seventy years had passed since King Henry VIII rescinded Tudor compliance with Roman dogma and founded a Protestant English church. Years of persecution followed, and not all of it one-sided. England was now Protestant, but a strong, stubborn Catholic element remained and was commonly assumed to be in league with Spain, which by then controlled most of the New World from South America as far North as Florida. 'Everybody thought there was a Spaniard under the bed,' said Ivor Noël Hume, 'and there were a lot of admitted Catholics, but many more closet Catholics, and I think that the Protestants felt that any Catholic was a potential spy.'

Hancock hypothesized that one of the settlers might have been a Catholic, a conspirator in an English or Spanish plot to undermine Protestant colonization of the New World. He visualized a murderous saboteur who poisoned the common food and water with arsenic. But anomalies continually overturn historical perspectives. It has commonly been assumed that early Jamestown was a wholly and staunchly Protestant settlement, but new archaeological evidence shows that Catholics were there, too. 'We have found artefacts reflecting Catholic iconography and it's been quite surprising,' said Beverly Straube, Curator of the Rediscovery Project. 'We were kind of shocked. There are bits of rosaries and some crucifixes and religious medallions showing the Immaculate Conception and that kind of thing. Not what you think of when you imagine Anglican Jamestown.'

It is true that as the deaths at Jamestown grew in number and frequency, the settlers became intensely suspicious of a threat within their own fortified walls. In 1607 one of the most capable administrators of the settlement, George Kendall, was accused of spying and was executed. 'The fact that they would do that,' said Ivor Noël Hume, 'suggests that the level of paranoia must have been really very high indeed, because you don't throw away one of your best men just because you think he may be spying.' But paranoia aside, was Kendall a probable spy? Hume doesn't believe so. 'I don't think there's anything to it, I think it was another of these stupid decisions to execute a man who was perhaps one of the most useful.'

It is tempting to surmise that the bullet in JR's leg was more evidence of the paranoia infecting the settlement, but whatever the case, the true inner workings of the tragedy at Jamestown may never be known. Hancock believes that someone must have been pulling the strings from England or Spain. Is it not really so far-fetched to believe in a plot to poison the first Protestant colony in America, given that a Catholic plot to blow up the English Parliament had so nearly succeeded a year before the colonists set sail for Virginia? When Guy Fawkes was interrogated about the gunpowder plot, the first person he named was a shadowy figure called Baron Thomas Arundel, a notorious plotter with an interest in alchemy and chemistry. Hancock's diligent research showed that not only was Arundel a fanatical Catholic, but he had a longstanding ambition to found a Catholic colony in the New World.

Hancock's discovery has been confirmed by Michael Barcroft, the Arundel family historian, who said, 'At the time when he thought there was the prospect of having an approved Catholic settlement, Arundel put up the funds for a boat called the *Archangel* under Captain Weymouth and a priest, a *Catholic* priest called Rosier, to go out to what was the coastline of Maine and northern Maryland on a reconnaissance expedition. It was extremely successful – short, sharp, and followed by very good propaganda. The *Archangel* returned with four Red Indians, and it was thought that they would be very useful in ensuring a peaceable landing of the first colonists.'

But the following year, when the chance to invest in the Virginia adventure arose, Catholics like Arundel were pushed aside. Later Arundel seems to have believed that the high level of prejudice had subsided and that he would at last be able to found a Catholic colony in the New World, but again, his hopes failed to materialize. 'He was deputed to be captain of an expedition which would include five hundred English Catholic soldiers and five hundred Irish,' said Michael Barcroft. 'They would go to the northern area and they would colonize it. And then that fell apart again, Arundel couldn't get a patent from the King. He was furious. It was then that he really determined to do his best to destroy Virginia.'

Indeed just months after the colonists arrived in Jamestown, one of Arundel's associates was arrested en route to Spain and charged '...with intent, and is thought to have betrayed his friends and show the Spaniards a means how to defeat this Virginian attempt.'

And Arundel's connections with the subject of poisoning are no less suspicious, as Barcroft relates. 'One of his associates, John Stanley, was arrested and confessed that he was going to spread a poisonous perfume around Queen Elizabeth and would kill her. The other person arrested at the time actually put poison all over the pommel of her horse.'

On one occasion when Arundel had been under suspicion in the 1590s, a telling reference to poisoning was found among his papers, as Dr Hancock noted. 'There are references to him having been interested in how to poison the air so as to infect an entire camp.'

Comprehensive poisoning of the Jamestown colonists would have suited perfectly the desires of Catholic Spain. Jamestown had been a serious irritant, virtually a symbol of failure on their part, for even though the settlement was outside their area of control, they nevertheless laid claim to the whole of the New World.

If Hancock is right, the poison plot was efficiently crafted to destroy Jamestown without the need for a military intervention, which would have been costly and could conceivably have provoked a fresh war with England. It could be significant that the only surviving sketch of the Jamestown fort, showing its exact location on the James River, was obtained by the Spanish Ambassador in London, Don Pedro de Zuniga, from his network of spies. It was found not in England but in Spain. In the Spanish archives there is also a letter from Ambassador Zuniga to King Philip III of Spain. It reflects Arundel's desire for revenge, and Hancock believes that it is self explanatory. Zuniga wrote, 'The truth is that they have failed to send him [Arundel] out because he is suspected of being a Catholic. He is actively discontented and he has told me that he will perform an extraordinary service in regard to this matter.'

'Baron Thomas Arundel was reported by Ambassador Zuniga to offer his services to Spain,' said Hancock, 'and that he would come to America and show them a means of de-establishing Jamestown.' Zuniga's actual words were, '...he will then tell your majesty how those people can be driven out without recourse to arms.'

Hancock believes this is a clear reference to a proposed poisoning plot involving militant Catholics; Arundel, however, may only have been a minor figure in an extensive plot involving England and Spain as they vied for control of the New World. The members of the Jamestown Rediscovery excavations do not accept Hancock's theory, but nevertheless it does mesh with the hostile manoeuvring of England and Spain at the time. It is also free of the anomalies inherent in traditional ideas about why the settlers died. There is strong evidence that they were starving; yet it seems there was food locally available. Why didn't they get it? They may simply have been too weak – it is widely thought that they were suffering from various diseases. But while Hancock accepts that hardship and deprivation may have contributed to the settlers' torment, his investigations have persuaded him that all their symptoms can be traced to arsenic. As an experienced pathologist he is convinced that this diagnosis is correct. He also believes that he has established not only the means of poisoning but the motive and, in Arundel, a credible conspirator in the plot. As matters stand, there is no other single-cause theory which puts forward such a structured explanation for the mysteries of Jamestown. 'I think the circumstantial evidence seems somewhat convincing,' Hancock says, 'and I think the literature available and the writings of that time need to be re-read and re-assessed from this point of view. I think the possibility of sabotage at Jamestown, both political and physical, is rather strong. And I suspect that the events will be proved.'

The few settlers who survived the horrors of the winter of 1610 were broken men. They abandoned Jamestown and set sail to find a more congenial place. A few miles downstream they met a supply ship from England and were persuaded to turn back. This time they did not simply survive; they began to grow crops, enough for themselves with enough over to feed new livestock. Little by little they thrived. Their numbers swelled and spread. A fresh start was forged from the early catastrophes of Jamestown.

It will soon be the 400th anniversary of the arrival in America of the first English colonists. That would be a fitting occasion for the writers of popular history to tell again the story of the settlers' suffering, incorporating the views of Dr Frank Hancock as well as those of more tradition-oriented investigators. It would also be a fitting occasion to grant the Jamestown colonists recognition as the true founding fathers of the United States.

2

BLOOD ON
THE ALTAR

THE ANCIENT PHOENICIANS WERE committed to
written communication, they developed writing as we know it and
actually invented the western alphabet, yet beyond a few scraps
and inscriptions, practically nothing they wrote has survived.
Their religious scrolls, their texts on architecture and seamanship,
their histories, inventories, genealogies, day-to-day chronicles –
the whole of their written legacy has gone. Great Phoenician
libraries at Carthage and Tyre were destroyed by the Romans and
Macedonians; countless other acts of historical and cultural
erasure, aided by the ravages of time, have ensured that not one
Phoenician manuscript exists in the original or as a translation. To
learn anything about this vanished civilization we have to rely on
the work of Greek and Roman authors and on biblical references.
'To the victor belong not only the spoils, but the tools with which
to rewrite the history of the vanquished,' said Glenn E. Markoe,
Curator of Classical and Near Eastern Art at the Cincinnati Art

Museum, who was recently commissioned by the British Museum to write a major study on the Phoenicians, the first for thirty years. 'It's through Rome's biased eye that we're forced today to interpret the story of the Phoenicians in North Africa.'

The ancient country of Phoenicia was a narrow strip of land on the coast of Syria, corresponding to present-day Lebanon. The chief cities of Phoenicia were Tyre, Sidon, Byblos and Arwad. Apart from their Semitic roots, the ethnic origins of the Phoenicians are obscure. We can't even be sure what they called themselves. The word 'Phoenician' was introduced by the Greeks, who based it on the word 'phoenix', which in Hellenic mythology was the name of a beautiful bird that lived for 600 years then burnt itself in a fire of aromatic twigs, only to emerge restored to vigorous youth, ready to embark on another 600 years of life. Scholars know the word has another meaning, however: it denotes the colour we call scarlet but which at that time was our colour purple, and the Phoenicians reportedly manufactured an expensive and much prized dye of that colour. The most likely name they gave themselves in ancient times was '*Ken'ani*', which translates as 'Canaanite'. As to where they came from, no one knows that either. Ancient tradition suggests they had their origins in the region around the Red Sea, but today's historical investigators view that as no more than an attempt to explain the Phoenicians' connection with the colour red.

The oldest system of government in Phoenicia appears to have been monarchical. Although the influential merchant families limited the king's power, the royal house had absolute claim to descent, and the monarch could not be chosen from any other line. The king was supported in his duties by a council of elders, at least that was the system adopted at Byblos, Sidon and perhaps Tyre. It is interesting to learn that although the Phoenicians kept themselves well ordered and regulated, they were not bound by any sense of national identity. Glenn Markoe explains that the cities of Tyre, Sidon, Byblos and Arwad were all staunchly independent, rivals who rarely worked in concert, except when they came under a common threat. Markoe further points out that although the Old Testament makes mention of Tyrians, Sidonians, Byblians and Arvadites, there is not a single reference to a Phoenician state or confederation. Such common ties as may have existed are not clear from surviving accounts.

They were conspicuously ambitious, and appear to have striven for supremacy in everything they tackled. When it came to establishing commercial dominance, the seafaring talents of the Phoenicians were indispensable. They are credited with the discovery of *Ursa Minoris*, the Pole Star, and with developing advanced techniques for its use in navigational calculations. They certainly lacked the advantages of electronic navigation aids, but their intelligence and ingenuity were often very fine substitutes. Dr Sebastiano Tusa, a marine archaeologist working on an excavated Phoenician ship at Marsala, in Sicily, explained an extraordinary discovery. 'We found bones in the vessel,' he said. 'These were analyzed and turned out to be the remains of two pigs.' That was surprising in itself, since the Phoenicians were a Semitic race and were forbidden to eat pork. 'I had heard stories about pigs being used by the Phoenicians to find land, as a navigational aid,' Tusa went on. 'We carried out an experiment to see if this could possibly be true. I would not have believed it if I had not seen it with my own eyes.'

Tusa put a tape into the museum video recorder. A film came up on the screen, showing a pig being thrown from a fishing boat into the sea. The beast swam vigorously with its snout pointing upwards. The shoreline was visible a long way off, and the pig seemed to be swimming in the wrong direction. Then quite suddenly an expanse of rock was visible above the choppy surface of the water. The pig headed straight for it and clambered out of the water on to dry land. 'Apparently pigs use their sense of smell to find the nearest area of land,' Tusa said. 'I say again, I would not have believed it unless I had seen it with my own eyes.' Incredibly, the Phoenicians had devised a system of radar roughly 3,000 years before Sir Robert Watson-Watt began his experiments.

Their nautical ingenuity aside, the Phoenicians were intrepid and patient navigators, sailing regularly into regions where no one else dared go, relentlessly seeking out fresh territories where they could develop commerce. In defence of their monopolies they always guarded the details of trading routes and new-found destinations, just as they kept secret their knowledge of prevailing winds and major sea currents.

The Phoenicians worshipped the god Baal, as did a number of Middle Eastern peoples. They apparently regarded him as a deity of fertility and one of the most important in the assemblage of all the gods. The word 'baal', surprisingly, was a Semitic common noun which meant 'lord' or 'owner'. But it could also be used much more widely than that: a baal of wings was a bird, while in the plural a ballim of arrows meant an assemblage of archers. Even so, the wide-ranging use of the word did not disqualify it from being applied to a god, who in Phoenician was sometimes called Baal Shamem – 'Lord of the Heavens'. Our knowledge of the personality, exploits and sacred role of Baal is drawn almost entirely from inscribed tablets excavated sporadically from 1929 onwards at Ugarit, which nowadays is called Ras Shamra, in northern Syria. The tablets, dating to the middle of the second millennium BC, seem to focus specifically on the worship of Baal at a local temple, but scholars believe the writings represent general Canaanite belief.

Fertility – and by extension, prosperity – was believed to have a duration of seven years before it had to be re-established. Baal, the god of life and fertility, engaged in bloody mortal combat with Mot, his most prominent enemy. Mot was the ancient West Semitic god of the dead and of all that stood against fertility and the breathing world; he was the son of the god El and the master of all things barren. If Baal were victorious in the struggle with Mot, a seven-year period of fertility would follow; if he was vanquished, there would be seven years of famine and drought. A variant tradition holds that Mot and Baal were perpetually caught up in a seasonal struggle which ended with Baal, like many similar harvest gods, being annually overpowered and killed. Mot, however, was also annually slaughtered by Baal's sister Anath, who thereby cleared the way for the resurrection of Baal.

But Baal was not every inch the fertility god. He is depicted as a deity of power, cunning, and diversity – as king of the gods, in fact (though not supreme god), who obtained his ascendancy by seizing divine kingship from Yamm, the god of the seas. A facet of Baal's cunning is apparent in the story of his desire for a palace which for opulence and grandeur would outshine those of any other god. He flattered the goddess Asherah and persuaded her to intercede with her husband El, the supreme god of the pantheon, to authorize the building of a palace. Kothar, the ancient god of crafts, then built Baal a magnificent palace which occupied an area of 10,000 acres.

The Phoenicians had their foreign admirers and detractors in roughly equal number. Among their more laudable characteristics were industriousness and high levels of technical accomplishment, as the Bible attests: 'And Hiram king of Tyre sent messengers to David, and cedar trees, and carpenters, and masons: and they built David a house.' (2 Samuel 5, 11).

They were a cultured people, many of them scholars and learned scribes. They were also innovators of an essentially practical kind, who developed efficient linguistic forms and devised systems of weights and measures. Their engineering skills were as formidable as their talent for building cities and creating fine works of art. They were eminent merchants, traders, voyagers, and dauntless explorers who colonized and imposed prosperity on numerous territories of the ancient world.

The city of Carthage in modern day Tunisia was the central gem of the Phoenician commercial empire. The site chosen for the city, centrally on the shore of the Gulf of Tunis, was considered perfect by Phoenicians, Romans and Greeks alike. It was erected on a triangular peninsula of low, undulating hills; at its rear was the Lake of Tunis, which provided secure anchorage and an abundance of fish. The city had natural protection because potential attackers could be seen while they were still far off. Defence was relatively easy, because the only possibility of land attack was where the southern end of the peninsula connected to the mainland via a slender strip of land. The ancient citadel, the Byrsa, stood on a low hill overlooking the sea, and some of the earliest tombs have been found there.

The city was a teeming commercial centre served by vast libraries, temples and law courts. The citizens lived in blocks of flats six storeys high, and the ruins of these and other buildings have recently been uncovered on the Byrsa Hill. Among those to be fascinated by the discovery was historian Glenn E. Markoe. He visited the ruins and found himself marvelling at the complexity and elegance evoked by the ancient remains. 'The city was an extraordinary architectural wonder,' he said. 'It would be amazing to be at Carthage two centuries before Christ, just to see the incredible residential complex of six-storey buildings looming up into the sky, feeling yourself dwarfed by the structures as you walked up the streets of the city. The six-storey building is extraordinary when you look at the normal house in the ancient world, which was a one-storey structure made of mud brick, with a very, very simple construction.'

Domestic life in pre-Christian Carthage was advanced beyond anything outside of Rome or Athens; as was the case with the Romans and Greeks, there was a clear emphasis on the hygienic side of everyday life. The basement levels of the apartment complexes at Carthage reveal massive underground cisterns with a capacity of more than 20 cubic metres which served up to sixty people living in each apartment block. Every apartment, moreover, had its own tiled kitchen and bathroom. In its golden day Carthage was so advanced that people came in large numbers, many of them from far-flung countries, simply to look and wonder at it.

But Carthage eventually fell victim to its own success. Jealous of the Phoenicians' commercial empire, first the Greeks and then the Romans waged intermittent war on them. Then in 264 BC, Rome launched the first of a series of concentrated military campaigns against the Carthaginians. These became known as the Punic Wars.

For 100 years the relentless force of Rome was resisted; the name of the Phoenician leader who commanded the Carthaginian forces against the Romans in the Second Punic War (218–201 BC) still evokes images of power and strength. 'Hannibal is the one Phoenician personality known to us today,' said Glenn Markoe. 'A great general of tremendous drive and stamina who crossed the Alps with a troop of soldiers mounted on elephants, and nearly brought the city of Rome to its knees. Had he done so, the whole history of the Western world as we know it today would have been written by the Carthaginians rather than the Romans.'

But in 146 BC, scarcely forty years after Hannibal's death, the Romans torched Carthage and destroyed it. A contemporary account by Polybius, a Greek statesman and historian who was at Carthage when it fell, graphically illustrates the terrible scenes of brutality and destruction. 'Some were stabbed, others were hurled alive from the roofs to the pavement. All places were filled with groans, shrieks, shouts and every kind of agony. Others were seen still living, especially old men, women, and children who had hidden in the inmost nooks of the houses, some of them wounded, some more or less burned, and uttering horrible cries. Others thrust out and falling from such a height with stones, timbers, and fire, were torn asunder into all kinds of horrible shapes, crushed and mangled.'

The Phoenicians were not only vanquished in battle; every trace of their traditions and their culture was systematically obliterated by their victors. As Glenn Markoe notes, 'The Romans' destruction led to the destruction of the great library at Carthage itself. As a result of that we've lost all of the original documents written by Phoenicians in their own language, describing what had actually transpired in that city in the years before the Roman destruction.'

In surviving Greek and Roman texts, written at approximately the time Carthage fell and in the years that followed, the impression is given that the talents and traits which won the Phoenicians respect in some quarters had earned them contempt in just as many others. They were depicted as tricksters and rogues beyond the reach of trust or decency; as hawkers and exploiters who swindled the unwary and kidnapped the helpless for ransom; as a race of morally bankrupt profiteers who had no qualms about turning their daughters into prostitutes. Worst of all was the accusation, actively supported in influential quarters to this day, that the Phoenicians regularly slaughtered infants in rituals designed to appease their gods.

Recently, eminent researchers have pooled their skills and considerable experience in an effort to determine whether child sacrifice really was practised by the Phoenicians. Their investigations, naturally, had to be carried out in the light of established historical facts, and there is certainly evidence that the ritual sacrifice of animals was a feature of the Phoenicians' worship of Baal. Consecrated upright slabs of engraved stone, known as votive stelae, bear descriptions of acts of worship involving the killing of animals. At the appropriate moment in a votive ceremony the creature to be sacrificed, commonly a sheep or a lamb, was led to the altar by the officiating priest, followed by lesser priests carrying ritual implements of slaughter, typically knives and axes. The animal was then killed and its body drained of blood. The head was cut off and laid on the altar and the body was burned on an open fire. During this time the officiating priest swung a censer over the severed head and intoned an offertorial prayer. After the animal's internal organs and its fat had been burned, the remaining meat was cut up and divided between the priests, who ate it. The beast's bones and ashes were then buried and a small dedicatory slab was erected over the grave.

Historians and archaeologists now agree that the ritual sacrifice of animals had an established place in the Phoenician calendar of religious ceremonies. But did they really go so far as to sacrifice infant children? Here the authorities disagree, and conclusive evidence for either side of the debate is hard to come by. Elsewhere, of course, there are solid grounds for believing that human sacrifice has been practised for centuries, usually with the aim of assuaging or forestalling the displeasure of a god or gods. There is a universal and long-standing human tendency to believe that plague, war, poverty, insanity and certainly death are the handiwork of supernatural forces; it is also human nature to believe that personal misfortune is the outcome of a personally generated affront, albeit unintentional, offered against the sacred being. The answer in general and individual cases is the same: to render oneself – or one's community – favourable again by means of sacrifice, bearing in mind that it operates on a sliding scale, depending on the severity of the offence. Atonement runs all the way from acts of abstinence or self-punishment, to the mass slaughtering of animals and even human beings. Sometimes a sacrifice is offered not to atone, but to obtain an advantage: it was common practice with the Romans of the Heraclius Dynasty to execute their prisoners of war in exchange, they hoped, for victory. In numerous parts of Africa, where human sacrifice was bound up with ancestor worship, the deceased person's slaves were buried alive with him; alternatively they were killed and laid below him in the grave. Among the Ashanti of southern Ghana, criminals and occasionally slaves were at one time sacrificed as 'first-fruit' offerings during the Festival of New Yams. In the part of Latin America that is now Mexico, thousands of men and women perished every year in the Aztec and Nahua calendrical maize ritual, slaughtered in the belief that the sun drew nourishment from spilled human blood. The Incas, on the other hand, resorted to mass sacrifice only on the accession of a king.

In spite of knowing that human sacrifice has been so widespread throughout history, many historians and other serious investigators still find it hard to accept the proposition that the Phoenician Empire, which at its height rivalled the civilizations of Egypt, Greece and Rome, could ever have been tainted by the abomination of child sacrifice. Glenn Markoe, an acknowledged expert on the Phoenicians, has no such reservations. He even puts forward a sacrificial scenario. 'We have this massive and very dramatic rite taking place in the dark, involving the cutting of the throat and bloodletting, accompanied by musicians... a blood sacrifice on the altar followed by cremation on a funeral pyre.'

Professor Larry Stager, an archaeologist and member of faculty at Harvard University, can supply detailed information about participants in the Phoenician rituals. He tells us, for example, that they had a Sacrificer, a specialist who was particularly adept with a knife and could slit children's throats very effectively.

Then there is Professor Piero Bartoloni, from the Cultural Institute of Phoenician and Punic studies in Rome, who doesn't believe any of it ever happened. 'In reality,' he says, 'child sacrifice never existed. It is a tale invented by the Phoenician civilization's many detractors down through the centuries, starting with the Greeks, then the Romans, all the way up to the twentieth century.'

Bartoloni dismisses the primary classical source of the sacrifice stories, Diodorus Siculus, as a purveyor of inflated hearsay. 'Siculus writes in the second century BC,' Bartoloni said. 'In his own way, he describes stories which he had only heard. This is evident, as he cannot have seen what he tells us, and it is clearly an imaginative tale. He tells us of a bronze monster with outstretched arms on which a child was placed, and would then fall down into a fire. He tells us of human sacrifices involving children up to eighteen years of age. Absolutely absurd things.'

Other sources, Bartoloni insists, are more important, 'and they are clearly more serious. [Writers] such as Polibius and Titus Livius, who wrote in that period of Phoenician history, didn't even mention human sacrifice. They didn't talk about a practice which, if real, would have been so important, so disruptive, that everyone in ancient times would have talked about it. By contrast with serious writers of ancient times,' Bartoloni said, 'Siculus was like the tabloid journalist of our time.'

History is written by the victors, so virtually everything we know about the Phoenicians was written by their enemies,

Greek and Roman, and in view of their open hatred of the Phoenicians, their accounts are often called into question. It must be said, nevertheless, that they have their defenders among present-day academics.

The Greeks wrote of fanatical and bloody religious practices where Phoenician men sometimes castrated themselves, in an attempt to be more like their goddess Astarte. She was, ironically, a goddess of fertility and for centuries she was revered and worshipped across the ancient world. A stout Norman castle now standing on a hilltop in Erice, Sicily, was at one time the site of the Phoenicians' vast temple to Astarte. Behind its walls, according to the Romans, the Phoenicians practised a ritual of sacred prostitution of their young virgins. 'It is an extraordinary and mystical place,' said Gaia Servadio, the author of a book about the Phoenicians in Sicily. 'People flocked here from all over the Mediterranean, it was a kind of Lourdes. And this was a place where sacred prostitution took place. The prostitutes were girls from what we would call good family, offering their virginity to the goddess Astarte.'

According to Roman and Greek historians, it was a regular event for Phoenician aristocrats to take their virgin daughters to the temple when they reached the age of puberty. Polybius observed, 'The girls had to go to the temple of Astarte and stay there and be lain with strange men...' The high priest would then make the girls have sex with wealthy visiting foreigners, who paid a substantial amount to the temple for the privilege. 'The stranger was viewed as an emissary for the gods,' wrote Polybius. 'After their intercourse the girl had made herself holy in the sight of Astarte, and went away home.'

'These young girls were actual prisoners until they were deflowered,' Gaia Servadio said. 'The pretty girls could get home quite quickly after giving up their virginity. The ugly ones had to wait to be chosen. Sometimes they might have waited for years and years. So these very young girls were not set free until they were deflowered. They waited until a rich Roman or a rich Etruscan came along – they had to be foreigners in order to take advantage of this offering to the supreme goddess.'

According to Greek and Roman accounts, sacred prostitution was also practised in Cyprus, Tunisia and Sicily. It was claimed that the Phoenicians exported their grotesque religious practices as they traded across the Mediterranean and beyond. Wherever they settled, they brought with them both their new skills and advances, and a few dark practices. By far the most repugnant was child sacrifice. 'In plights of great danger,' Polybius wrote, 'it was a custom of the Phoenicians to give freely their beloved first-born children in sacrifice as a ransom to the avenging demons. Those given up were slaughtered in mystic rites...'

Gaia Servadio has an interesting aside on the matter of sacrificing the first-born. 'My own feeling is that the rather dark practice of sacred prostitution could be linked to the Phoenicians' other dark aspect, child sacrifice. It could be that the husband, the man who would eventually marry the girl who had been a prostitute at the temple, might think that the first baby was not his own. It was the fruit of the foreign visitor, and was therefore expendable. But that would only happen if it was a boy, of course, because the girls would be spared, because child sacrifice we think was only of the first born, especially at the beginning, and only a boy.'

The record goes on to say that emergencies aside, the Phoenicians sacrificed their children principally to appease their bloodthirsty gods, Baal Hammon and his wife Tanit. Baal and Tanit took a number of forms: they could have animal faces or be human; Baal was often represented as a disc and crescent, Tanit as a triangle with added upward-reaching arms. Today some commentators believe Baal was the root of the word Beelzebub (in the Bible, Baal-zebub) which became one of the many names for the Devil.

According to both the Greek and Roman accounts, the ceremony of child sacrifice began with the parents handing over their baby to the high priest to be anointed with perfume and oils while the Sacrificer made preparations for bringing about the baby's death. The priest carried the baby at the head of a procession, bringing it to the sacrificial altar in a sacred precinct known as a Tophet. Grinning masks have been found in Phoenician sites associated with religious sacrifice. It is probable they were hung on walls to ward off evil spirits in the next world, but some experts believe they were worn by the parents to hide their grief. Even the Romans, not known for their humanity, claimed to be shocked at a religious ceremony where babies had their throats cut. Pliny the Elder lamented, '...they would bring to the altars children whose age evokes pity even among enemies. To think that men were so barbarous, so savage, that they gave the name sacrifice to the slaughter of their own children.'

An unidentified Greek chronicler wrote that the dead baby's face became like one of the grinning masks when it was thrown on to the funeral pyre. 'When the flames fall upon the body the limbs contract and the open mouth seems almost to be laughing. Thus it is that the "grin" is known as sardonic laughter.' As the cremation proceeded, the chronicler went on, 'the whole area before the statue was filled with a loud noise of flutes and drums so that the cries of the wailing should not reach the ears of the people. They sometimes sprinkled the children's blood upon the altars, and thus implored the favour of the gods through the blood of those sacrificed.'

The quantity and detail of the Greek and Roman accounts of child sacrifice has meant that for hundreds of years they have generally been accepted as largely factual. But nineteenth-century historians increasingly began to dismiss these sources as biased and unreliable. The fashion swung, but there are still those who believe the Roman and Greek accounts in spite of others, like Professor Pierro Bartoloni, quoted earlier in this chapter, who say it is all an elaborate and extended smear campaign.

But Glenn Markoe can't agree with that. 'While it is clear the Phoenicians were not well loved among the Greek and Roman peoples,' he said, 'it would be very difficult just to toss aside all these citations and say they are completely tendentious and have no root in actual fact.'

The decades of academic argument intensified and took on new perspectives when archaeologists, excavating at Carthage, uncovered a Phoenician sacred precinct – a Tophet. Underneath standing stones that looked similar to gravestones, they found hundreds of urns containing the charred remains of human infants. A number of authorities now believe this is a site where the ritual sacrifice of children actually took place. 'You might wonder why a sophisticated people, among the most sophisticated in the Mediterranean or even the world at that time, would have indulged in such a barbaric practice as child sacrifice,' said Professor Larry Stager, who led the international team that fully excavated the Carthage Tophet in the 1970s. 'I don't pretend to have all the answers, but I do think they practised child sacrifice on an institutional level.'

They exhumed 20,000 urns. The sheer mass of what they had uncovered was astounding. 'We had maybe twenty thousand over a two-hundred-year period in ancient Carthage that we would estimate were sacrificed. That's about – oh, what is it? – a hundred year at least.'

The situation was crying out to be explained. What is this place the archaeologists had found? Did parents really take their children there to be ritually slaughtered, or did the Tophet have a much more innocent purpose? Professor Bartoloni believes it did. 'The Tophet is simply a separate place,' he said, 'isolated from the adult cemetery, where stillborn children were buried, or those who died soon after birth. It is important to remember that in ancient times seven out of ten children died in infancy. Of the three who survived only one would reach adulthood. So infant mortality was extremely high. And these dead children were buried in an honourable way to appease the God and to help to bring on another pregnancy.'

The Tophet now forms the core of the debate over whether the Phoenicians did or did not sacrifice their children. Matters would be helped forward if the precise function of the Tophet could be established – was it an ordinary children's cemetery or a ghastly setting for ritual human slaughter? 'The archaeology doesn't prove anything one way or another,' said Professor Stager. 'We can't say whether it was actually child sacrifice, with the remains then being buried in special burial grounds, or whether it was simply children dying of natural causes, being cremated, placed in jars and buried in these special precincts. It's an arguable question that hasn't been resolved to everyone's satisfaction, otherwise we wouldn't still be arguing about it.'

In the 1970s forensic archaeology was still in its infancy. Huge strides have been made and now, finally, new scientific techniques may be able to settle the argument once and for all. 'What we are able to do today,' said Stager, 'is quite a bit more than we could have done twenty years ago, when analyzing what are probably the most important elements of this archaeology, namely the physical anthropology – the bones of the cremated or burnt children.'

During a three-month period in the year 2000, scientists in Britain and Israel used advanced forensic techniques, together with equipment at its then-current state of development, to analyze the charred remains of children exhumed from a Tophet. Early in the summer a team of distinguished British scientists, accompanied by Glenn Markoe, travelled to Motya, a small island off the coast of Sicily, 100 miles north of Carthage. A team in Israel, meanwhile, were preparing work on bones from the Tophet at Carthage.

In Phoenician times Motya was a peninsular city with over 15,000 inhabitants. In 397 BC, however, it was destroyed after an extended siege. The inhabitants were massacred and the buildings left to decay. That disaster proved a huge benefit to the team: Motya was never fully re-populated, so unlike the site at Carthage it has never been cluttered and obscured by the debris of successive civilizations. Markoe said, 'This site is significant first of all because of its contrast to all of the other cities that the Phoenicians occupied, which were always in such amazing locations that they were built upon by the Romans and by people after them. Because of the remarkable condition of the site, we have a number of complexes that are *completely* preserved. One of them is the Tophet.'

Archaeologists discovered a large walled precinct in Motya, just as the team at Carthage did, and they excavated 6,000 clay urns. These, like the others, were filled with charred bones. All of the urns discovered on the island were carefully placed in store-rooms where they were kept under lock and key. Only the scientific team would have access to them.

Dr Charlotte Roberts, a biological anthropologist, had to decide if the remains were sufficiently well preserved to indicate the children's state of health immediately prior to death. If the bones showed evidence of disease then it would be likely the Tophets were ordinary cemeteries for children who died from natural causes. Indications of normal health, on the other hand, would go some way to supporting the hypothesis that these were the bones of children who had died unnaturally. Dr Roberts's task was complicated: the bones were over three thousand years old, they had been burnt, and they were badly fragmented. Her task would have been greatly simplified, she pointed out, if there had been whole skeletons to work on. 'You can find out a lot about the person and the person's life if you have a complete skeleton,' she said. 'Potentially, you could work out the sex of the individual, assuming that you have the pelvis, which is the most identifiable area that relates to the sex of the person. And with a youngster you can work out quite accurately the age at death. It gets more problematic when a person becomes an adult, because all the bones have developed, so have all the teeth, and people start degenerating at different rates depending on who they are and what their lifestyle is.'

Determining the sex of an adult from the bones is relatively straightforward, Dr Roberts emphasized, but with a child there are serious obstacles. 'If you've got an adult skeleton, yes, potentially we can find out the sex, but a non-adult skeleton, one that's not actually developed totally, a person who hasn't reached puberty, it's just impossible with the methods we have to determine the sex of that individual. But we can start to look at aspects of health, although only the diseases that actually affect the skeleton. I think that with our archaeological skeletons, we're perhaps only seeing a small proportion of the people with disease, because a lot of the diseases affected only the soft tissues. So ideally, that's what we could find out if we had a complete skeleton.'

But at Motya Dr Roberts had only the burnt and fragmented bones from the urns to work with. Nevertheless she was able to say straight away that the bones were indeed from infants, and in spite of the fact that most fragments were little larger than 2 or 3 centimetres in length, she could identify particular bones, such as a part of a lower jaw, a rib, and a breast bone. In several cases she also found what is known as the petrous part of the skull's temporal bone, which contains the structures of the inner ear; this portion is remarkable for its hardness and density, and it usually survives cremation rather well.

Not all of the fragments proved to be human. There were pieces of pelvic bones and slivers of shin and rib which had come from either sheep or goats. They were identifiable by their cortex or outer coating, which is much denser in animals than in human beings. There were the bones of birds, too. Many of the urns excavated at Carthage in the 1970s also contained a mixture of animal, bird and human bones, and the evidence can be interpreted in different ways. No one disputes that the Phoenicians sacrificed animals in the Tophet, and one theory is that animals and children were occasionally sacrificed at the same ceremonies, their cremated remains subsequently becoming mingled on the funeral pyre, and then in the burial jars. 'It's unlikely that this is an intentional interment in the jar,' said Larry Stager, 'but just an accident of scraping off the pyre.'

In the view of other academics, however, the mingling of human and animal bones was no accident. They believe the Phoenicians sacrificed animals and birds when they cremated new-born babies who had died of natural causes. Piero Bartoloni, on the other hand, believes that it was standard practice for a child's body to be accompanied by that of a bird or animal, by way of companionship, on the journey to the next life. That might explain the urns with mixed remains, but many of the urns from Carthage contained only animal bones – Larry Stager cited one that contained only the bones of a lamb. 'So,' he said, 'my question to those who claim that this is just an infant cemetery that is only for children who died of natural causes, is why in the world are they burying their pets?'

Among the fragmented bones heaped in the urns at Motya, Charlotte Roberts discovered human teeth, which can be a valuable indicator of general health. 'The teeth survive very well during burial,' she said, 'much better than bones, so we do get quite a lot of evidence for dental disease, what we term metabolic diseases or disorders of normal metabolism, things like anaemia, rickets caused by a deficiency of vitamin D, and scurvy, which results from vitamin C deficiency.' Metabolic disorders affect dental development even in children whose teeth have not yet erupted through the gum. After careful scrutiny of the tooth enamel under a microscope, Charlotte Roberts was prepared to voice a conclusion. 'On the basis of what I have seen, there are no defects in the teeth from these individuals, suggesting that they didn't suffer any disease or nutritional problems.'

In all, Charlotte looked at the remains of more than twenty children. She found nothing to suggest that any of them died of disease. There is also a piece of archaeological evidence at Motya which supports the theory that the children in the Tophet were healthy when they met their death. It is an engraving on one of the standing stones found above the urns. 'It is a very evocative image,' said Glenn Markoe. 'It actually shows a priest cradling a young infant in his arms. I think it's very clear that the child is alive, is being held upright and cradled in the arm and I think this was the process that preceded the immolation of the child, the cutting of the throat and the actual sacrifice.'

Markoe believes that the stout Phoenician wall surrounding Motya provides further archaeological evidence of the special status of the Tophet. In Phoenician times Motya was connected to Sicily by a road. Although the road is underwater now, an area of lighter blue in the lagoon which isolates Motya shows the position of the road very clearly. The presence of that thoroughfare made Motya vulnerable to attack from the mainland, and when the Greeks declared war against the Phoenicians in the fourth century BC, a defensive wall was hastily put up around the island.

'Now, the wall itself,' Markoe said, 'because it hugs the contour of the island, cuts across the cemetery and literally bisects it.' To save time, the wall's builders took the easiest route even though it meant erecting it across the cemetery. However, when they came to the Tophet they took the trouble to build around it. 'The implication of this, of course,' said Markoe, 'is that it was very sacred hallowed ground. What we have is not a cemetery for children who died from natural causes, but a very sacred precinct of ritual child sacrifice.'

Markoe may be right, but he admits that only unambiguous scientific evidence would prove conclusively his belief that ritual child sacrifice was a Phoenician practice. 'I think the evidence that would really settle this debate would be evidence of the age of the children cremated.'

The age of the children when they died is critical because Professor Bartoloni maintains that the Tophet is simply a special cemetery for infants who died naturally before they were born, or soon after. To quote him: 'So the Tophet, what is it? It's an open air space where Phoenician children, either stillborn or who died soon after birth, were buried.' If the children who were cremated were shown to be older, this would suggest that this wasn't the case.

How old, then, were the children cremated at the Tophet? In theory, the teeth discovered by Charlotte Roberts were capable of providing an answer – at least they might tell her the ages of her sampling of approximately twenty cases. 'We know in modern populations how the teeth develop,' she said, 'when each tooth starts to grow, when it comes through the gums and shows in the mouth. We can therefore compare what we see in our archaeological teeth, with the modern data.'

An examination of the state of eruption of the deciduous teeth (usually called milk teeth) of infants gives a reliable indication of age in most cases, because the times of eruption of the different teeth are fairly constant. It has to be remembered, nevertheless, that these early teeth can appear abnormally early, and in a few cases a number of teeth have been visible at birth; similarly, their appearance can be abnormally delayed. The twenty deciduous teeth appear between the sixth and ninth month and the twenty-fourth month of life. They are shed, on average, during the twenty-four months between the fifth and seventh year. In the case of teeth no longer lodged in the skull, their individual characteristics – enamel and dentine development, crown formation, configuration of root, overall dimensions – can be noted and used to arrive at a reliable age for the individual who possessed them in life.

The teeth examined by Charlotte Roberts indicated that none of the twenty children had been stillborn or new-born. All of the teeth were from infants aged between two and three months old. Shortly afterwards, even more fascinating evidence came from Israel, where the Hebrew University in Jerusalem had a team analyzing the teeth found in Carthage. Once again the aim had been to determine the age of the babies in the urns. In late summer 2000 the preliminary results on the tooth samples came through. In the report the samples were referred to as tooth germs: a tooth germ is the entire sample, consisting of the external enamel organ and its inner structure of dentine (the ivory forming the mass of the tooth), making up the whole tooth at its arrested stage of development. Thus far in the investigation, none of the babies had been found to be stillborn. Professor Patricia Smith, a physical anthropologist on the team in Israel, identified samples showing deaths at the age of two or three months. But she also found teeth from older children. A two-thirds formed crown of a first permanent molar indicated that the child had been approximately two years old at the time of death. 'We have so far only looked at a small sample of the remains from Carthage,' said Professor Smith, 'but already we have found some infants who were as old as five years.'

Not one of the forty children examined from both the Carthage and Motya Tophets was found to have been stillborn. Their ages ranged from two or three months to five years. Clearly, these results undermine Professor Bartoloni's theory that the Tophet was a special cemetery for stillborn children or those who died shortly after birth. But up to this point, nothing has been demonstrated that is substantial enough to vindicate either side of the argument. In these areas of debate opinions are easier to encounter than hard facts, but one further forensic test could conceivably settle the debate: DNA analysis. Until now, DNA has never been successfully extracted from the cremated remains of people who died 3,000 years ago, although it has been taken from much older bones which were not cremated. But with the broken, incinerated remains from the Phoenician Tophets, there is powerful incentive to try. Only DNA testing will confirm the sex of the dead children, and it is important to know this, because according to biblical and classical accounts, the children sacrificed were exclusively male:

They have built also the high places of Baal, to burn
their sons with fire for burnt offerings unto Baal...
(Jeremiah 9, 5)

But some scholars have cast doubt on the accuracy of the translations. Glenn Markoe is one. 'Sometimes they refer to boys but I think that's a generic term for children as a whole. There are certainly no references at all to young girls being involved in the sacrificial process.'

If the children died of natural causes their numbers would be made up from both sexes. But if the skeletons in the urns all turned out to be boys, the case for child sacrifice would be considerably strengthened. Feasibility was discussed among the experts and it was eventually decided that specialists would attempt to extract DNA from samples of bone from the Tophets. Professor Larry Stager was keen that the attempt should succeed. 'We would be able to determine whether or not it is a male or a female that is being sacrificed and this will be of great interest, especially since at least some of the biblical details and other classical references at times imply that it is first born males that are chosen to be sacrificed.'

Professor Bartoloni was sceptical. 'If these tests show us for sure that these children are the first born, that they are exclusively boys, I'll eat my words. But I don't think they will.'

Dr Ron Dixon and Dr Keri Brown are internationally renowned microbiologists who took up the challenge to extract DNA from the ancient bones. There were daunting barriers to the success of the attempt, but Keri Brown believed that certain inefficiencies in early methods of cremation might work to the advantage of herself and her colleague. She spoke of experimental work done by a colleague at the Wessex Trust for Archaeology. 'She carried out a series of experiments where she tried to recreate what a Bronze Age pyre might have been like, using a carcass of a sheep instead of a human being. The sheep was placed on a fire of logs which had been arranged in a way that would create maximum heat. Then she put thermocouples in the pyre and inside the body of the sheep.'

A thermocouple is a thermometer fashioned from two wires of different metals joined together at one end. The opposite ends are kept at a constant temperature within an electronic readout box containing a millivoltmeter – that is, a meter capable of responding to tiny electrical voltages. The joined ends are fitted into a fireproof probe which can then be applied to an object or substance whose temperature has to be measured. Heat acting on the joined wires produces voltage, which is interpreted by the millivoltmeter as a measurement of temperature. 'She found that in the flames, the temperature got up to over a thousand degrees centigrade, but inside the carcass of the sheep it didn't even reach three hundred degrees – it was somewhere between two hundred and fifty and three hundred degrees – which is not very high. That's quite an inefficient cremation procedure. Probably what happened was that the fleece of the sheep, and the fat and the flesh, protected the bones, so there's probably a good chance that DNA survived in those bones within the carcass of the sheep.'

If the cremations carried out on the children at Motya had been as inefficient as the experiment suggested, then there was some hope of locating DNA of usable quality. 'If we can get DNA out of these infant remains, and if we find sequences from the Y chromosome, we have a male infant,' Keri Brown said. 'If we just get DNA from the X chromosome, we've got a female infant. This would be the way forward to finding out whether we've got boys and girls being sacrificed, or not, as the case may be.'

Chromosomes are fundamental to the success of any project aimed at determining gender from tissue that is no longer alive. Chromosomes are groups of genes, which themselves are portions of DNA (deoxyribonucleic acid) which has been called the circuit diagram of life. Genes are the basic components of heredity, and the string of genes that make up a single chromosome is often depicted as a string of beads, although in nature it takes the physical form of strings of genes wrapped in a double helix around a protein core. Every species of plant and animal life has a precisely individual number of chromosomes – human beings have twenty-three pairs. In each pair, one chromosome comes from the mother and one from the father. The forty-six chromosomes in human cells hold a single sex-determining pair: in males it's an X and a Y chromosome, in females a double-X pair. Detection of the appropriate pairing is essential to determining sex from a DNA sample.

At Motya, the human bones whose structure had best survived the cremation process were the ones most likely to contain ancient DNA. Ron Dixon and Keri Brown made their selection from the jars in the warehouse and bagged the samples ready for transportation back to England, where the attempt would be made to extract DNA. 'They're *very* fragmented,' said Keri Brown, 'and there's a variety of colours, some of them are very dark, some of them are pale, indicating they were exposed to different temperatures during the cremation process. What we'd like, of course, are the bones that have been less cremated, less exposed to the burning process, and hopefully the DNA will have survived within these bones. So we need nice thick chunks of bone where there's been some protection from the flames.'

Although there were realistic doubts about being able to isolate any DNA from these less-than-perfect specimens, Keri pointed out that DNA could be tenacious stuff. 'I think we're certainly within the time limits,' she said. 'DNA has been extracted from Neanderthal bones that were at least thirty thousand years old. These are only three thousand years old. So they're well within the survival limits for DNA.'

The handling and transferring of the bones from their urns to plastic bags was done with great care, and in near sterile conditions. Ron Dixon explained why. 'We take extraordinary precautions – gloves, masks, and so on, and all the packaging material is sterile, because we want to protect the bones from our own DNA. We produce DNA on our skin and we could well contaminate the bone samples.'

Dixon was pessimistic about the possibility of extracting DNA from the bones, in spite of the fact that it is so abundant in nature, particularly in human beings. 'People contain huge amounts of DNA in their bodies,' he said. 'If you could unravel the DNA from the billions of cells that we normally contain, then that DNA would stretch to the sun and back a hundred and twenty nine times. Of course when we die, this is rapidly degraded into very small fragments, perhaps no larger then your thumbnail.'

Back in England, at Bradford University, Ron Dixon and Keri Brown spent weeks struggling to extract DNA from the remains they had brought from Motya. Try as they might, they could locate no traces. One place where tiny fragments of truly ancient DNA sometimes survive is in the teeth, but the microbiologists' hopes in that direction evaporated early on. 'The teeth were really badly degraded,' Ron Dixon said. 'We were left with only the enamel shell and we know, being realistic, that we're unlikely to get DNA from that sort of material.'

The other specimens were also in a much worse condition than Keri Brown had hoped. 'The bones don't seem to be very well preserved at all,' she said. 'They don't seem to have anything by the way of microstructure. By microstructure I mean the little channels through the bone matrix which carry things like blood vessels. And of course it's from these little blood vessels that the DNA comes.'

In spite of the unpromising realities the researchers were not about to give up. They carried on trying, day after day, supervising research assistant Alex Whan as she subjected samples to the procedures which would yield DNA if there were any to be found. At all stages of the time-consuming work, meticulous care was taken to ensure there was no contamination of the specimens. Alex Whan worked alone in a sterile environment, gloved and gowned and wearing protective goggles. Before testing each tiny bone fragment, she had to cut off its exterior surfaces to remove the DNA of anyone who might recently have handled the fragment. It was then put in a test tube to which was added a chemical solution which would react with the bone and draw out any available DNA. Each time she performed this action, she added the same solution to an empty tube as a control. 'It's very important while the extraction from the bone is carried out that there's also a parallel extraction,' said Keri Brown. 'In other words, you go through exactly the same procedure but with no bone present. If that control gives you a positive result then you know there's DNA contamination getting in somewhere – for instance from the researcher.'

Once the solution had been added to the bone the tube was shaken thoroughly, then put into a water bath with a temperature of 60 degrees Celsius. This procedure was designed to help leach out any residual DNA. Following that the tube was placed in a centrifuge, a high-speed rotating device used to separate the bone fragments from the solution which, by that time, would contain any of the ancient DNA that might have resided in the sample. Finally Alex Whan drew off the solution, using a pipette. The entire process took twenty-four hours, at the end of which Whan was left with only a tiny amount of clear liquid. Checking to find out if it contained any DNA involved yet another lengthy process.

'Since one of the characteristics of ancient DNA is that very little of it survives,' said Keri Brown, 'we use what's called a polymerase chain reaction – PCR – to target a particular piece of DNA.' PCR is a technique for making large numbers of copies of a specific segment of DNA, using an enzyme, polymerase, to speed the process. The chain reaction takes place in a machine which puts the DNA sample through various cycles of heating and cooling, alongside the action of the polymerase, to effectively magnify tiny fragments of DNA until they are big enough for analysis. Because DNA from a very broad range of sources can be amplified in this fashion, the technique is regularly used in a number of fields. In clinical medicine PCR is used in the diagnosis of genetic diseases, and to uncover minute levels of viral infection. It is also used in forensic medicine to analyze tiny traces of blood, semen and other materials, so that the donor may be identified by his genetic 'fingerprint'. The technique is used to enlarge DNA fragments discovered in preserved tissues, and to uncover the genetic make-up of extinct animals found preserved in permafrost and ice.

The fluid residue from the Motyan bone samples was subjected to a PCR routine designed to magnify any traces of DNA a billion times. In order to find out if any DNA is present, the PCR-treated samples have to be stained in a special gel and viewed under ultraviolet light. 'If we located a male,' said Keri Brown, 'we'd see two bands. One would be from the X chromosome, one would be from the Y chromosome. If it was a female we would see just one band because females have two X chromosomes.

'When we look at a gel under ultraviolet irradiation, hopefully we should see some bands with ancient DNA which will tell us whether we're dealing with male or female infant remains.'

Alex Whan went through a genuine test of endurance, working on the samples day in and day out, taking the most lavish care to ensure there was no contamination and no variation in the agonizingly slow stages of the process. Keri Brown appreciated the level of dedication. 'For Alex it has been a real struggle with the extractions and the PCR, and running the gels to get results from these bones. If she succeeds in getting any results from the samples, it'll be a heroic effort on her part.'

Each attempt to extract DNA took three days. After twelve failures the team were hoping that number thirteen would be lucky. But it was not. At that point Ron Dixon was prepared to make a statement. 'We now know that we really can't find DNA that will survive a cremation in this type of bone.'

Even so, Alex Whan wanted to make one final attempt, and she persuaded Keri Brown and Ron Dixon to let her.

Meanwhile in Jerusalem, Professor Pat Smith had managed to extract tiny DNA fragments from the bones taken from the Tophet at Carthage. 'We do have some preliminary results,' she said. 'They all show two bands. So it seems that, at least for the specimens we've looked at, we have boys. Obviously we need to look at a very much larger sample before we can say definitely that the probability of girls being buried there was extremely low.'

If it could be shown that the babies' remains in urns found in the Motya Tophet were also boys, then science would have gone some way towards proving that the Tophets were sites of ritual child sacrifice.

Back in Bradford, Alex Whan had gone through another three-day cycle of testing and was about to find out if she had managed to uncover ancient DNA. She had summoned Ron Dixon and Keri Brown for the moment of truth. When they looked at the test gel they found, incredibly, that she had done it. The gel showed a clear presence of ancient DNA, alongside modern DNA for contrast and comparison. 'That's marvellous!' Ron Dixon was openly delighted. 'And it's a girl!'

A moment of triumph, without doubt, but it was a disappointing result for those who argued that the Tophets had been places of child sacrifice. Professor Larry Stager said, 'I don't want to make too much of that evidence until it's been further studied and we continue to do more work on these bones, because we're still learning more even though it's now several decades since we did our excavations in Carthage.'

The Israeli team are now embarked on a massive study, planning to conduct DNA tests on 2,000 infants from the

Carthage Tophet over the next five years. If they find a reasonably even mix of both boys and girls, Professor Bartoloni's stance would be reinforced considerably, and Roman and Greek accounts of child sacrifice would lose much of their credibility. But the advocates of the child sacrifice argument see no reason to abandon their stance. 'If we find a great predominance of young girls,' said Glenn Markoe, 'this would fit in with the bias that we might have in the ancient world of young girls being undervalued by society. So it would be easier and less painful for the family to sacrifice a girl than a boy. If boys were predominant, then this would fit in with the supreme sacrifice of the young first-born male.'

The absence of disease in the teeth, and the ages of the skeletons analyzed so far, suggests that child sacrifice did indeed occur. But the discovery of a female child has thrown these findings into confusion. Science and human ingenuity move forward, however, and age-old mysteries are being unravelled every year. For the first time, scientists in Britain and Israel have demonstrated that ancient DNA can be extracted from bone fragments cremated and buried nearly 3,000 years ago. There is no reason to doubt that over the next few years, given the rate of scientific progress, we may finally know if the Phoenicians were the victims of vicious libel, or if indeed their sacrificial altars were stained with the blood of children.

3
MURDER AT STONEHENGE

IN ADDITION TO THE damage caused by 4,000 years of weather, natural degeneration, souvenir hunting, and vandalism, the Stonehenge that visitors see today has suffered large-scale theft of its stones by builders of the medieval and early modern periods. Generally described in guide books and encyclopaedias as a prehistoric monument, Stonehenge is thought to have been built from approximately 3100 BC onwards, and was erected in successive versions known as Stonehenge I, II, and III, the final one erected in phases, ending about 1550 BC. Modern interpretations of the site are founded on excavations carried out since 1919 and particularly those since 1950.

The monument stands 8 miles north of Salisbury in Wiltshire and is made up of several elements, most of them circular. A ditch 321 feet in diameter runs around the outside, and immediately within it there is a bank. Small circular ditches enclose two flat areas on the inner side of the bank, called the

North and South Barrows. The major ditch and the bank inside it are cut through at the north-east, creating a gap, which is the pedestrian entrance to the monument. At the centre there is a horseshoe arrangement of tall upright stones cut from sarsen, a sandstone still found scattered across the chalk downs of Wiltshire. A ring of similar sarsen uprights, all of which were originally topped by lintels of the same material, although only a few lintels now remain in place, encircles the horseshoe. Inside the horseshoe there was once an arrangement of hefty bluestones, foreign to the area and eventually identified by archaeologists as spotted dolerite (similar to basalt), which it is presumed were brought from the Prescelly Hills in Pembrokeshire. The bluestones were removed some time after 200 BC. Other stones still at the site, named centuries ago for what was presumed to have been their purpose, are the Slaughter Stone, the Altar Stone, and two Station Stones; the Heel Stone, which stands on the pathway outside the main area of the monument, is bedded firmly into the ground and tilts or 'heels' towards the entrance at the north-east.

In creating Stonehenge I, local neolithic (Stone Age) people dug an approximately circular ditch 321 feet in diameter by 20 feet wide by roughly 6½ feet deep. The chalky rubble excavated in the process was used to make a high bank inside the circular ditch. The builders also put up two parallel entry stones on the north-east of the circle – the surviving Slaughter Stone is one of them. Inside the circular bank a circle of fifty-six shallow round holes were also dug, and the evidence suggests they were filled in again almost at once. They were called the Aubrey Holes, after their discoverer John Aubrey, the seventeenth-century antiquarian and writer. Stonehenge I was used for approximately 500 years, after which it reverted to overgrown land.

When Stonehenge II was built, about 2100 BC, the site was comprehensively remodelled. At its centre eighty bluestone pillars, each weighing roughly 4 tons, were set up vertically to form two concentric circles which were never completed. The entranceway to the bluestone structure faced sunrise at the summer solstice, around 21 June, the time when the sun is highest in the sky at noon; the alignment was extended along a newly built and wider approach, called the Avenue, flanked by a pair of Heel Stones over which the sun could be watched rising at the appropriate time of year.

The raising of the linteled circle and the horseshoe of sarsen stones, whose remains we can see today, marked the opening phase of Stonehenge III in approximately 2000 BC. The sarsen stones were brought 19 miles north from the Marlborough Downs and erected in a circle of thirty uprights topped with a circle of stone lintels. Within this ring was then erected a horseshoe formation of five triliths, each consisting of three stones, two upright and one resting across them as a lintel. The tallest of the sarsen uprights still standing is 29 feet high and weighs 50 tons. The lintels are held in place on the uprights by mortise and tenon joints made with hammers; the lintels of the circle fit together with tongue and groove joints made by the same simple means, and although the tools were basic the work is remarkably accurate and detailed. The lintels are cut to a curved shape to produce the overall effect of a smooth circle; the pillars taper towards the top, which gives them a very stable appearance, as well as enhancing the perspective effect when they are viewed directly upwards from the ground.

The second phase of Stonehenge III followed within a century of the first. This time twenty bluestones from Stonehenge II were set up in an oval arrangement inside the sarsen horseshoe. Later there was an elaborate scheme involving two concentric rings of holes, not visible today, which were dug outside and surrounding the sarsen circle; it has been deduced from the size and number of these holes that the plan was to erect the sixty remaining bluestones from Stonehenge II inside them, but the plan appears to have been abandoned and at approximately the same time the oval setting in the centre was dismantled. The holes were left open and allowed to silt up naturally.

The final phase of building in Stonehenge III is believed to have followed almost immediately after the second phase. A horseshoe arrangement of roughly twenty hammer-dressed bluestones, alternating a pillar with a pointed obelisk followed by a pillar and so on, was erected within the sarsen horseshoe. Midway between the inside of the sarsen circle and the outside of the sarsen horseshoe, the remaining sixty or so unshaped bluestones were arranged as a circle of pillars. Rebuilding appears to have stopped at that point, although in 1100 BC the Avenue was extended eastwards for a stretch and then south-eastwards to the River Avon, a distance of almost 1¾ miles, which is a good indication that Stonehenge was still in use at that time.

But what was Stonehenge *for*? There is no record of why it was built, nor any explanation for so many painstaking revisions. The eighteenth-century antiquarian William Stukeley was the first to observe that the openings of the horseshoe of triliths and the horseshoe of bluestones faced squarely in the direction of sunrise on Midsummer Day. It therefore followed, he believed, that the monument had been deliberately crafted and meticulously aligned so that at dawn on the solstice, the sun would rise unerringly over the Heel Stone, and its very first rays would shine directly into the centre of the double horseshoe. This suggested to Stukeley that serious ritualistic sun worship had been practised in pre-Christian Britain, and that Stonehenge had probably been erected as a temple to the sun.

Stukeley's discovery, and the inferences he drew from it, enjoyed enormous popular appeal, and strongly affected the way Stonehenge was perceived and interpreted for many years afterward. At the beginning of the twentieth century the influential astronomer, Sir Norman Lockyer, wrote a treatise on Stonehenge which supported and built upon Stukeley's view of the site as a centre of mystical worship. In 1963 an American astronomer, Gerald Hawkins, went further when he claimed that in addition to Stonehenge being passively aligned with the midsummer sunrise, it had an active and more important function; it could be used as a predictor of astronomical events such as solar and lunar eclipses. In other words, Hawkins believed Stonehenge was an astronomical computer. It must be said that the majority of Stonehenge archaeologists have argued strongly against Hawkins's thinking on this topic.

There has been just as much resistance to other well-publicized theories about the purpose of the site. In 1649 John Aubrey wrote that the Druids, ancient Celtic priest-magicians, were probably responsible for building Stonehenge and using it for the performance of religious and magical rites. He later devoted a chapter to the topic in his influential *Monumenta Britannica*. In the early eighteenth century Aubrey's speculation became known to

William Stukeley, who was impressed enough to help spread the notion of Druidic involvement in the mystery of Stonehenge. This romantic theorizing, popular as it was in Stukeley's day, has never been accepted by serious students. All the evidence points to the fact that Stonehenge was in existence for hundreds of years before the advent of the Druids, whose earliest recorded existence dates only from the third century BC. R.J.C. Atkinson, an archaeologist from University College, Cardiff, summed up the view of many objective investigators when he said, 'Most of what has been written about Stonehenge is nonsense or speculation. No one will ever have a clue what its significance was.'

But if the precise meaning of Stonehenge itself lies beyond the reach of investigation, there are related mysteries that can yield startling insights into early British history if the investigator is patient and determined enough. Mike Pitts is a Stonehenge specialist and an expert on the neolithic period. As a practical archaeologist he has conducted a number of excavations in the shadow of the stones, and recently set out to tackle a mystery that has remained unsolved since 1923. On 3 November that year, more than three years into the largest excavation ever undertaken at Stonehenge, Lieutenant Colonel William Hawley uncovered the skeleton of a man buried in a shallow grave a few yards south of the stone circles. Mike Pitts hoped to link the resources of archaeology and forensic science to find out who the dead man was, when he lived, and how he died. 'Stonehenge is unique,' said Mike, 'Anything buried in the ground there has to have had a special significance, and there has to have been something very strange and special about the fact that people chose that particular spot to bury that particular man.'

Ancient human remains had been found at Stonehenge before, but this find was different; it was the first complete skeleton ever to be exhumed at the site. It had been found crammed into a single shallow grave less than 2 feet deep; intriguingly, the head lay at right angles to the body and appeared to have been severed.

In 1923 the skeleton was racially typed by a technique (now discredited) which relied upon identifying race through skull shape, and it was catalogued as a British man from the Roman period. That much having been established to the archaeologists' satisfaction, the bones were boxed and put into storage at the Royal College of Surgeons (RCS) in London, where they were believed to have remained until 1941, when the college took three direct hits from German bombers during the Blitz. Its archives were blown apart and scattered, many of them lost or completely destroyed. There was no record of the mysterious skeleton from Stonehenge having survived the bombing, and, until very recently, it was presumed to have been obliterated before modern science could make an evaluation.

Mike Pitts's curiosity was first sparked when he came across official documents that suggested that certain archives from the RCS had in fact been moved before the bombs fell in 1941; it seemed possible that the skeleton had survived the air raid and could be lodged with other skeletons from the RCS collection now resting in the vast basement storerooms of London's Natural History Museum.

That was how the investigation began. Naturally enough, the first thing Mike wanted to do was track down the skeleton. He approached the authorities at the Natural History Museum who took the relevant details from him and then, thanks to the diligence of members of staff, the appropriate cardboard boxes were located, four of them, in a cupboard where they had lain practically undisturbed for sixty years.

Now Pitts had to make sure that the bones in the boxes really were the Stonehenge skeleton, so he called on the expertise of an osteo-archaeologist, Jackie McKinley, who is an authority on ancient human remains. With great care Jackie McKinley set the bones out on a table and gradually reassembled the skeleton, which was now being called by its catalogue name, '4-10-4'. Once the bones had been assembled in proper anatomical order, Jackie McKinley made a detailed examination of the skeleton, checking her findings against the relevant archaeological notes of Lieutenant Colonel Hawley. In the end she found no ambiguities as far as verification was concerned: several distinct features of the bones matched precisely those mentioned in the notes, confirming this was the skeleton Hawley had disinterred at Stonehenge in 1923. 'At the time of 4-10-4's death,' Jackie McKinley said, 'he had been a healthy man, about 5½ feet in height and approximately thirty years old.' 'He's not a big, butch chap,' she added. 'I don't think he'd done a lot of weightlifting.'

There was some indication of how he had died. Jackie McKinley showed Mike Pitts the appropriate bones as she explained. 'These are the neck vertebrae.' She held them in column formation, roughly as they would be in life. The top bone, the atlas, was the one 4-10-4's head would have rested on, while the second, which had a long round-ended protrusion jutting upwards from it, was the axis bone on which the atlas would have rotated. 'When you get to the fourth one down it's not quite all there.' Jackie McKinley pointed to where a clean oblique slice had been taken off the top of the vertebra, the angle rising from the back of the bone to the front. 'It's gone right across the hole in the middle,' Mike Pitts observed, 'so it would have gone through the spinal cord.' Jackie McKinley agreed. 'So,' Mike concluded, 'if he wasn't already dead, he would certainly have been after that blow.'

The emerging scenario was already dramatic; a beheading had occurred at Stonehenge, possibly in Roman times. Jackie McKinley took the fourth cervical vertebra – the one with the cut – and the bone above it, holding them with her thumb and forefinger, maintaining a space between the two. 'I'm going to try and hold them the right distance apart. Obviously, there is a space between them, because you've got to remember there was the intervertebral disc in there.' The leading edge of the cut on the lower vertebra was visible in the gap between the two, a space that in life would have been occupied by a spongy, fibrous-coated, shock-absorbing disc. Although the gap between the bones was slight, the lower edge of the upper bone was not damaged. This led Mike Pitts to speculate that the blow which made the cut had been from a very thin blade. Again Jackie McKinley agreed, 'It looks more like a blade than something really hefty like an axe.' 'Something more like a sword or a machete,' said Mike.

The cut did not appear to go all the way through the fourth vertebra. That, in addition to there being no visible damage to the vertebra immediately above, suggested that the instrument delivering the blow had not gone all the way through the neck but had stopped where the oblique cut ended, just short of the front of the fourth vertebra. 'By that point it had gone through the spinal cord, anyway,' said Jackie McKinley. The weapon had scythed through flesh and bone, and though it may not have completely separated 4-10-4's head from his body, he would have died at once.

With the method of the man's death tentatively established, Mike Pitts decided the next thing he needed to know was when this man had died. He paid a call on English Heritage, the caretakers and guardians of Stonehenge, and asked them if they would carbon date a sample of bone from 4-10-4. They agreed, but warned him the process was time consuming and would probably take many weeks. Until then, Pitts had to consider a broad time sweep. 'We can see from the wound that the man was killed with a very sharp, probably steel, blade,' he said. 'We don't have those in, for the sake of argument, 200 BC. It's certainly not contemporary with Stonehenge, which is four thousand years old. On the other hand, if he were killed in an historic period, we'd expect to have a written record of that. So we can say that he died before the Norman Conquest, before 1066. We have this broad span of time within which this man might have died. And other things being equal, it seems to me the most likely context within that time span is going to be early Roman.'

Roman pottery and coins found around the grave supported the original cataloguing of the skeleton as Roman British, and the presence of the artefacts seemed to indicate some kind of activity at Stonehenge during the Roman period. The Romans, under the emperor Claudius, invaded Britain in AD 43. It was not the first time: Julius Caesar invaded in 54 BC, and in later years his adopted son Augustus, who would become the first emperor of Rome, extended many of the aid-associated relationships Julius had developed with warring British tribes. This gave Rome a foothold in Britain, albeit a shaky one.

When Claudius came it was with the intention of occupation, a decision he took partly from ambition, partly from a need to suppress British tribal aggression, which undermined the stability of long-term alliances between Rome and Britain's principal indigenous powers. The occupation lasted nearly 400 years, and for much of the time it was characterized by conflict and violent death as the invading legions collided with ferocious tribal opposition. Near Stonehenge, tribes such as the Durotriges to the north and Dobunni from the south often clashed with the Romans, and there are records of summary executions being carried out by the occupying legionaries.

Mike Pitts identified three plausible explanations for a beheading at Stonehenge during the period of occupation. Evidence of all three can be found nearby at Cirencester, a place rich with the imprint of Roman Britain. There is documentary and archaeological evidence of decapitation in battle, judicial beheading, and the severing of the head as a funeral rite. Deaths in the first and second categories were commonplace; contemporary accounts by the Roman historian Tacitus, possibly the greatest prose stylist to write in Latin, speak of Britain as a complicated jangle of war-painted, chanting tribes against whom battles and terminal punishments were frequent. So Mike Pitts wondered if 4-10-4 had been a casualty of a battle between invading Romans and British tribes. Chris Knusel, a biological anthropologist from Bradford University, was invited to comment.

'When someone is decapitated in battle, it's usually not with a precision strike and the death-blow will come at a very unusual angle,' he said. 'It will be directed more at the head and neck, and the neck just happens to be that entity which catches the main force of the blow. There will also probably be evidence of previous injuries on the body, injuries that would have perhaps disabled the individual, followed by head, face and neck injuries that were meant to extinguish that person's life.'

Apart from the sliced fourth vertebra, the skeleton of 4-10-4 showed no other signs of trauma, apart from a small nick on the jawbone. 'Now what this would suggest,' said Jackie McKinley, 'is that this individual wasn't attacked – it wasn't part of a skirmish. Other decapitations I've seen that are obviously from that kind of scenario have various other cut marks on the skeleton as well, because in those cases people don't make just one blow. There tends to be a series of blows.' Minimal injury to 4-10-4's body indicated nothing so much as a single, clean, lethal blow to the neck, and to Jackie McKinley that suggested an execution.

Mike Pitts had two other possibilities to consider, one of them being the ritual decapitation performed at some Roman funerals. Five per cent of skeletons excavated at Roman cemeteries, including some found at Cirencester, show evidence of this ritual. 'Some of those decapitations were done from the front,' said Chris Knusel. 'They were done with multiple strokes of a small tool – usually looking like a knife of some description, and it suggests more of an *incising* motion. When the head was removed, it was actually placed in the grave out of alignment and in an unusual position, usually at the foot end of the burial, between the shins or the thighs, or maybe at the feet.'

Acts of this kind are thought to have been rituals of care and respect for the dead. While no one can be sure of that, there is some speculation that they were usually performed following a sudden death, the removal of the head being intended to liberate the soul from a body unprepared for an abrupt demise. However, since key features of this graveside ritual are the way the head was removed from the front, and with a number of carefully incising strokes, this procedure did not match the evidence from 4-10-4, where a single blow landed on the back of the neck.

Some time was spent speculating and theorizing on how the fatal blow was applied. Angle, in particular, would seem to be an important indicator of the relative positions of victim and attacker at the moment of death which, in turn, could strongly indicate the nature of the confrontation. The difficulty with estimating the angle of the blow from the attacker's standpoint, however, was that 4-10-4's skeleton gave no indication of his body position at the moment of impact. 'It looks like what's happened is, the blow has come up from this direction into the back of the neck,' said Jackie McKinley, indicating a sharp upward sweep. 'That is assuming the victim is upright of course – which at the moment, we are not sure about.'

In spite of lingering uncertainties and quite a few unknowables, the evidence made it highly unlikely that a burial ritual was the cause of 4-10-4's beheading. Mike Pitts was therefore left with only one explanation for a Roman beheading at Stonehenge: an execution.

Mike visited an early Roman site with Professor Michael Fulford, a Roman archaeologist from Reading University. 'If I had sat here, eighteen or nineteen hundred years ago,' Mike said, 'could I have actually seen a beheading?' Yes, he could, said Professor Fulford. Public executions almost certainly took place at amphitheatres like the one they were standing in at Cirencester.

'And what would have been the occasion with an event like that?'

'Probably it would have been a judicial execution,' said Professor Fulford. 'That would be the most obvious explanation. A court hearing in the town, the governors come and the trial is held; decision, execution. And, of course, we've actually got the skulls here, in the cemetery just a few hundred yards from the amphitheatre, which bear out the fact that something like this might have taken place here.'

Written evidence exists from approximately the time of the beheading at Stonehenge, revealing that the Romans publicly executed the leader of a northern French township. This led Mike to wonder if 4-10-4 had been a local leader or some other person of importance at the time of the Roman occupation. Perhaps he had even been the leader of an indigenous tribe, singled out for exemplary punishment. 'It's like doing detective work, really,' Jackie McKinley said, 'except you don't have any witnesses to help you.'

But even without witnesses, solid forensic evidence can still be assembled. Radio-carbon dating of 4-10-4's skeleton would – it was hoped – reveal when he lived and died. As insurance in the dating process, two bone samples had been taken rather than just one, and that was a fortunate precaution, because something went wrong with the first sample. At the point when the dating process was about to begin, Dr Christopher Ramsey of the Radio-carbon Laboratory at Oxford University explained the position. 'At each stage of the chemical pre-treatment, we do various quality-control checks to test that the yields and the ratios and so on are exactly what we would expect, and of the two samples, one of them has passed all those checks and one of them hasn't. So, I hope that we will get a result, assuming that nothing goes wrong at a later stage with the remaining sample.'

Mike Pitts, meanwhile, was trying to firm up the proposition that 4-10-4 had been an indigenous tribal leader executed by the Romans. If that had been the case, then the man would have been born in Britain, so nationality was the first fact to establish. A premolar tooth from 4-10-4's jaw was extracted for analysis. When soil and mineral samples from the grave area were set against the residual chemical information from the tooth, there would be a good chance of finding out where the deceased had originated.

Mike Pitts went along to the gravesite to collect an earth sample. He pointed out how much shorter the pit was than the body it had accommodated. Lieutenant Colonel William Hawley's original excavation diary noted how the body appeared to have been unceremoniously crammed into the narrow scrape. It was less than 2 feet deep, carved out of chalky soil.

'This is pretty tough,' Mike Pitts said as he started to dig into the rocky ground with a long-shafted, two-handled core extractor. 'I guess when they dug the grave all that time ago it wasn't a pleasant job. They would have been using spades, possibly pickaxes, and they would have hit this stone in the same way that I have. They might have been in a hurry. Who knows? Maybe the man himself had to dig the hole. It was not long enough to take his body and they were clearly in a hurry to get it over with. I suppose it wasn't a pleasant job for anyone.'

The earth sample, Mike explained, was to provide a control for comparison with the analysis of the bone. 'In a normal excavation, we would have just excavated the grave and we'd take some soil from the grave fill. But in this case, of course, the entire grave was excavated in 1923 so we no longer have any of the fill. We are just getting a sample that's close by.'

When he finally managed to twist out a representative specimen from the ground, Mike put on latex gloves, carefully opened a small plastic bag and took out a screw-top specimen bottle. 'This little container has been specially cleaned in the laboratory so that it is completely uncontaminated. I'm going to stick it right into the centre of the core of the soil, so we can get a clean sample.'

Meanwhile, the specimen of enamel from 4-10-4's tooth was going through the final stages of preparation for analysis. Hopes of a successful outcome were high: in spite of the problem with one of the two bone samples. It remains true that in most cases heavily enamelled pre-molars can be relied upon to trap information about an individual's geographical origins. 'Teeth are very resilient,' said Janet Montgomery, an archaeological chemist at Bradford University. 'They survive very well in the ground. Often in archaeological burials they're *all* that survives and they also resist any contamination. So we can be fairly confident that when we analyze a tooth we are actually getting something that was put there while the individual was alive, rather than something that's been incorporated from the soil after burial.'

The isotope ratios that characterize the particular tooth are first of all established, then they are compared with various geologies until one is found which ties in with the biochemical profile provided by the testing. 'The geology of the United Kingdom is very diverse and varies widely across quite a small scale. So you can move from one area, say on the South Downs, up to the Midlands, and be living on a completely different geology – the isotope ratios derived from your food and water would be very different.'

While the tooth analysis went ahead, some intriguing new information was being unearthed. Twenty-five years before Mike Pitts located 4-10-4's bones at the RCS, a now-deceased dentist and amateur archaeologist called Wystan Peach had come across the skeleton at the Natural History Museum and had paid for his own private carbon dating of a tiny sample of bone from one of the boxes. At that time it was not realized that the skeleton in question was the same one Hawley had exhumed in 1923.

Carbon dating results in the 1970s were far less specific than now and they were often unreliable. While no scientific records remained of Peach's test result, a couple of letters were found at the Natural History Museum and one of them offered Mike a different time-perspective on his mystery.

At the museum Professor Chris Stringer showed Mike the row of file boxes where old correspondence was stored. He opened one of them. 'These are a couple of letters from twenty-five years or so ago.' He fished them out and passed them to Mike. They were on Wystan Peach's headed notepaper, with the address of his Cardiff dental practice. 'I recall Wystan Peach coming here,' Professor Stringer said. 'He was a nice old chap, very enthusiastic, and as I recall, his request to us concerned a skeleton from Stonehenge. He wanted it to be absolutely dated by radio-carbon. And in his letters, clearly he was asking us about the sampling. We permitted him to take a sample for dating at Harwell, which he was prepared to pay for, and they came back with what he gives here as a provisional date. The date they got was AD 760.'

'Well…' Mike studied the letters, nodding, 'this is a real tease, because on the one hand it looks like a precise date, but on the other hand without the details and with this word *provisional* included in it, to me it's actually saying that I can't even assume now that the period was Roman.' Mike had been all but convinced that 4-10-4 was the victim of a Roman execution at Stonehenge and still expected the radio-carbon dating – still underway at that point – to prove he was right. But the Peach letter meant he now must at least consider a later, Anglo Saxon, killing as a possibility.

That called for a significant jump forward on the historical timeline, from a period of organized if turbulent daily life to a time of relative disorder. When the Romans left Britain in the fifth century their largely cohesive influence diminished and the fabric of British life crumbled. It was the beginning of a chaotic loss of national identity, a time in Britain of desolation and social decay; it was the spiritual and intellectual nightfall that historians called the Dark Ages. Centuries passed before British society began again to embrace positive values and strive to regain a sense of community. This massive reversal was brought about largely by the Anglo Saxons, Germanic settlers who laid the new foundations of law and order in the seventh century.

While readjusting his speculation about the long-dead man from Stonehenge, Mike Pitts remained practical in his efforts to learn more; whether 4-10-4 was from Roman or Anglo Saxon times, one reasonable certainty was that he had been executed with a thin, sharp blade. Mike believed it would throw more light on the mystery if he knew just what that weapon had been. Annoyingly, the predominant weapons in both the Roman and

Anglo Saxon periods were fitted with thin, sharp blades – in Saxon times it was the broadsword, in the Roman period the shorter and lighter gladius.

Perhaps practical experiments with both weapons would narrow the probability in one direction or the other. The person to consult on this matter was Dr David Sim, an experimental archaeologist and specialist in swords at Reading University. Remarking on his long-standing interest in these weapons he said, 'Swords are weapons that have fascinated people ever since they were first made. They do have special capabilities. The archangel Michael used a sword. Swords are given names, they are imbued with mystical powers, even kings carry swords. They appeal to something right at the heart of all of us and there is a magic about them. You've only got to pick one up and you can feel it. It empowers you and it protects you as well.'

Dr Sim has worked in experimental archaeology since 1969. It is a discipline, he explains, where no end is ever reached; each fresh piece of research generates new avenues of enquiry. 'An experimental archaeologist is there to try and fill in the gaps that can't be filled by any other method but experiment, particularly when one is looking at manufacturing processes. We very often have the end product; we very often have the waste products. What we don't have are records of how those processes were carried out. The role of the experimental archaeologist is to try and find that out. You can't ever say at the end of an experiment that this is definitely the way that it was done, but what you can do is eliminate almost all the other possibilities, so that what you are left with is a high probability of the way it was done.'

Turning to the question of what killed 4-10-4, Sim said, 'If you think about an execution being carried out in the time period where this individual was most likely executed, it's probably an execution that was done on the spot. There was no great preparation. If you wanted to decapitate somebody, and axes weren't a normal part of your equipment, then you'd have to use whatever came to hand. A sword would be the weapon of choice.' He was quick to point out that, in combat conditions, the efficiency of a sword depended on the skill of the man wielding it. 'But against an unarmoured opponent,' he said, 'you could take a head off without too much trouble.'

In this case 4-10-4's damaged vertebra showed a clean cut which did not completely sever his neck. This could have had some bearing on the type of weapon used in the execution. David Sim assembled an armoury for testing – it included a Roman gladius and a Saxon broadsword. On this occasion a succession of sheep necks, fresh from the butcher, were mounted on a bench, ready to take the blows. 'If you want to see how a weapon works, you need to replicate as closely as you can what a human body looks like when it's alive. You need bone that has still got the marrow in it. You don't need the flesh particularly but you do need the bone. Try a weapon out on fresh bone and see what effect it has, not only on the bone, but on the weapon itself, because sometimes you can make a weapon with a nice sharp edge, you strike a bone with it just once and it turns the edge. Right away you know that *that* kind of configuration is not what you want for a battle weapon. Remember it's designed for killing people. That is its main function. It's not just designed to do it once, either, it's got to be able to function well for the length of the battle, which would perhaps last a day or so. At the end of it the weapon can be repaired.'

Sim first tried an axe, which cut through the sheep's neck easily with a single blow. 'When you swing an axe,' he said, 'you generate an enormous amount of energy. It would go straight through a human's neck and I feel it would probably cut through two without any trouble at all. From what I know of the characteristics of the wound we are looking at it's not the kind of wound that would be produced by an axe.'

The gladius was designed primarily as a short one-handed stabbing sword and was the standard weapon of Roman legionaries. Could it deliver the power to decapitate? David Sim put it to the test. 'The gladius is quite an easy weapon to use,' he said. 'It's remarkable that when I struck double-handed then single-handed blows, the amount of penetration was almost the same. That surprised me quite a lot. Certainly, if you couldn't take a head off in a single blow with the gladius, you could cut seven-eighths of the way through.' So it could have been the Roman gladius.

The next contender, the broadsword, was longer and heavier than the gladius, and it had been the main weapon of Anglo Saxon warriors. Again Sim applied the sheep's-neck test. 'Broadswords were certainly the easiest to use,' he reported. 'Anybody who was reasonably skilled with a sword could take a head off without any trouble at all.'

What was his conclusion? What weapon was used to put 4-10-4 to death?

'I think it would be impossible to say, actually, *definitively*, that it came from this period or that period. You can't make a hard

THE JAMESTOWN MASSACRE

LEFT • Captain John Smith, settler and friend of Pocahontas. He survived to record the gruesome deaths at Jamestown.

BELOW • Reconstruction of the Jamestown fort. An orderly exterior belied the horror of early days on the peninsula.

ABOVE • Ancient Carthage, heart of a culture whose history was
systematically erased and rewritten by the Romans.

ABOVE • The Tophet at Motya. Six thousand clay urns were recovered, packed with the bones of children.

RIGHT • Baal, stern god of the Phoenicians. Did they appease him with ritual child sacrifice?

ABOVE • Dr Jackie McKinley with
the blade-damaged vertebra of the
skeleton exhumed at Stonehenge.

LEFT • Tacitus (AD 55–117),
eminent scholar who described
first-century Britain as a jangle of
war-painted chanting tribes.

ABOVE • George Viccars's cottage, where Eyam's plague
arrived in a parcel of cloth.

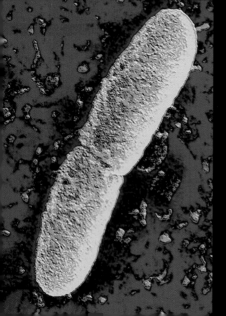

ABOVE • A rat flea, carrier
of the Black Death.

LEFT • *Yersinia pestis*, an ancient
bacillus possessing features in
common with HIV

LEFT • Medieval plague victim. Once the diagnosis was confirmed, treatment was less important than isolation.

THE REAL ZULU DAWN

ABOVE • The battle of Isandlwana, a massive British defeat

ABOVE • The redcoats'
prized Martini-Henry .45
rifle. During modern
testing it overheated
and jammed.

LEFT • Credo Mutwa, a
high medicine man. Zulu
were not warmongers, he
said, but they were good

and fast assessment of exactly what weapon was used from what period. If you look at something like the edge that's on a sharpened gladius and the edge on a broadsword, they are virtually identical. You can't prove that either of them was the weapon used in this case just by looking at the cut that it produced. It could have been either of them.'

Even though the weapon could not be pinned down, Mike Pitts still hoped to find out how the beheading took place. The aforementioned nick on 4-10-4's lower jaw, at the outer angle below the left ear, presented a possible clue. Jackie McKinley demonstrated. When the jaw and the injured vertebra were anatomically aligned – first to represent the deceased in an upright position, then to simulate kneeling – the nick on the jaw and the damage to the fourth vertebra were in alignment. 'But it's a matter of what the scenario was,' Jackie McKinley said, 'whether it happened all in one go.'

'Do you think it could have?' Mike asked her.

She nodded, 'I think it could.'

So hypothetically the combination of wounds suggested two possible positions for the body just prior to death: standing or kneeling. The kneeling position powerfully suggested a controlled execution.

Jackie McKinley tried to extend the hypothesis and give it more substance. If the victim had been standing and had been attacked from behind with the weapon travelling at a probable upward angle, the impact might feasibly have caused his head to turn a fraction and receive a glancing blow at the angle of the jaw, just as the blade sliced into the fourth cervical vertebra. By going through the possible stages of the beheading methodically and without haste, and by checking the probabilities at each point, Jackie began to see problems with the theory that the victim had been kneeling. 'I don't think the head could have been down,' she said, 'because if the head was down you would probably have got more damage on the mandible than you do have. Standing straight, that fourth vertebra is on a level with the mandible and as I suspect, the head's moved up and slightly across which is why you've just got this nick on one side.'

Alternatively, if the head had been down when the death-blow landed, it was likely there would have been much more severe damage to the mandible. Although Roman judicial executions are commonly thought to have been carried out with the victim kneeling, Jackie did not discount a standing decapitation; in fact she favoured that likelihood over the alternative.

Mike hoped to prove his theory of a controlled beheading by assembling a team of experimental and forensic archaeologists to work through all of the possible scenarios of 4-10-4's death. From the start, the group challenged Mike's theory that the victim was kneeling with his head forward. Gathered around a fully articulated artificial skeleton, placed in a kneeling position with its hands tied behind its back and its head pushed forward, they delivered their verdicts.

'There isn't a way,' said Dr David Sim. 'I don't think that you can produce a wound on this set-up which has got the same characteristics as the wound on the existing skeleton.'

Dr Sarah King, an archaeologist from York University, agreed. 'If you were executing an individual, you would expect the blade to go straight down. What we have is the vertebra sliced at an angle.'

Malin Holst, an osteo-anthropologist from Bradford University, said, 'I think that we can conclude that the blow was definitely from behind and the torso was upright or standing.'

The upward angle of the cut in 4-10-4's fourth cervical vertebra swayed the group towards the view that he was standing upright when the blow fell. If the victim was standing, perhaps even moving away from his attacker, then it is possible he wasn't the target of a controlled killing at all. Mike's theory was sinking to its knees until sword expert David Sim, having weighed up the evidence, voiced a misgiving. 'I'm not happy that this was done when he was standing,' he said. 'If he was standing upright you'd have to get your sword up here...' He held the sword at shoulder height, 'and you can't get any energy behind it.' Chris Knusel agreed. 'The minute your hands go above your shoulders, you lose power in the swing.'

After a few test sweeps with the sword held at shoulder height and higher, Sim was in no doubt at all and said flatly, 'Your arms and shoulders are in entirely the wrong position to get any energy behind the weapon you are using.' He went on to suggest that 4-10-4 was probably kneeling with his head upright. That way, the man wielding the sword had the angle and thrust to effect a decapitation. The execution theory held up.

'I'm convinced,' said Mike Pitts. 'You have a victim who is kneeling with a straight back. He can't run off. Somebody approaches him from behind, quite fast, maybe a step or two forward with a very sharp sword. Instant death.'

David Sim elaborated on that, 'They'd probably meant to decapitate him but they missed slightly.' He demonstrated with a one-handed sideways swipe from behind the skeleton, 'So the blade passes through his neck, it kills him, takes the bit out of his jaw and his head doesn't actually come off, but it's going to fall forward.' 'And so,' Malin Holst said, 'that would explain why he was buried the way he was, with the head at a right angle to the rest of the body.'

The scenario had grown more vivid and convincing for the gathering of experts. 'Maybe he just fell on his face,' said Mike Pitts, 'and they dug a hole just beside where he lay and kicked him into it.'

So they were agreed: the forensic evidence pointed to an execution, but at that point, without a probable date for the event, no one could say if it was Roman or Anglo Saxon.

'I keep wondering what sort of man this was,' Mike Pitts admitted. 'I like to try and visualize his face, his personality and his dress. But without a date I have to stop myself getting too clear in my mind exactly who he was and what he was doing. That is going to profoundly affect the context of the individual, the sort of person he was.'

Almost a year to the day after Mike rediscovered the Stonehenge skeleton, he learned that he would soon find out when 4-10-4 was executed. Prior to learning the verdict he said, 'I've got my ideas about what I think this date should be, based purely on archaeological judgement, but I admit there is virtually no hard evidence whatsoever, so it's pure intuition, and intuition, of course, goes wrong, so the date is going to be something else. It's kind of exciting and I'm nervous.'

Mike had no doubts about the validity of the result he would be given. Contemporary radio-carbon dating is sophisticated and precise and he knew it would reveal a date pinning the execution at Stonehenge either to a specific period of Roman conflict or one of Anglo Saxon order.

The big day came and Mike went along to see Dr Peter Marshall at English Heritage, who held out a sheaf of papers to him. 'I know you've been waiting for this for some time,' he said. 'These are the results from Oxford of the radio-carbon analysis.'

Mike stared at the top sheet, the words swimming before his eyes. He blinked a couple of times and read the date range. 'A Saxon,' he breathed.

The calculated time of 4-10-4's execution was between AD 620 and 770, therefore Mike was investigating an Anglo Saxon beheading. Theories involving the Romans were abandoned as he set about placing the skeleton in the later Anglo Saxon period. Although he had been given a time span of 150 years, he believed it might be possible to pinpoint the date more closely than that. All living matter contains carbon, a proportion of which is radioactive and starts to diminish or decay after death. Carbon dating measures the decay and provides an estimate of the period within which death occurred. But tree rings known to date from specific years can also be analysed for radioactive carbon.

Mike made the necessary arrangements at Oxford, and when the results from known-age tree rings were compared with data from the Stonehenge bone sample, a probability curve was produced which pointed to a much more closely bracketed date for the execution. Dr Christopher Ramsey of the Radio-carbon Laboratory at Oxford University summarized the results on the graph. 'We can see from this that the tree rings which match most closely to the radio-carbon date we've obtained are the ones in the middle of the seventh century.'

The graph peaked at a very significant period in Anglo Saxon history, the years between AD 650 and 690, forty years which marked a time of great change. Christian belief was making inroads on a pagan society. At the time of the Stonehenge beheading, lavish pagan burial sites like the one at Sutton Hoo in East Anglia were being transformed from the resting places of kings to the darker purpose of burial sites for social outcasts. The new Christians hoped that interment at these special sites would guarantee eternal damnation for the deceased. 'What really surprised us was the finding of some burials which were very plain, just bodies placed in graves,' said Professor Martin Carver, Sutton Hoo Research Director at York University. 'There were no grave goods. They were buried crouching, kneeling, and lying on their backs with arms in the air. And the heads – some of the heads were off and some of the heads were by the knees and some of the heads were in the right place, but the wrong way round.'

In all, thirty-nine burials were found at Sutton Hoo, and there was evidence that gallows had once stood on the site. 'The burials were in a ring,' Professor Carver continued, 'and in the middle of the ring were four post sockets, so we thought ha! What must have happened here is that these people had been killed. It came in with the Christian kings, they punished them [outcasts] twice: firstly by killing them and secondly by burying them in a pagan burial ground. It's as though to say, right, you step out of line and you are not coming in with the new Christian kingdom, we bury you there. We bury you in the pagan burial ground.'

Until recently experts had no evidence to show that Stonehenge had been used for any specific purpose so late in its history. But in the light of the findings at Sutton Hoo, it was tempting to speculate that the pagan significance of Stonehenge gave it a sinister purpose under the new Christian Anglo Saxon order of the seventh century.

According to Sarah Semple, an archaeologist from Queen's College, Oxford, the position of 4-10-4's burial and the treatment of the corpse clearly indicated he was an outcast. 'It's a person who is being taken away from society and buried in a place outside of society's limits. We are seeing a clear image that Stonehenge has become associated with fearful and superstitious ideas. A place where a deviant can be executed and buried, and it would say about the person that they have been a wrongdoer of some sort, and potentially of some significance.'

So the next line of conjecture presented itself: what had 4-10-4 done to justify an execution at Stonehenge in the late seventh century? Major social changes at this time were not solely religious. It was a period when land ownership on a grand scale was beginning, and with this came the law codes, detailing the first laws of an emerging nation, protecting property and punishing wrongdoers.

'The law codes describe a range of offences, and what you've got to do to make up for what you've done, in incredible detail,' said Dr Andrew Reynolds, a medieval archaeologist at University College, London. 'For example, the earliest Kentish laws of about AD 600 say that if you are walking along the street with a spear over your shoulder and you poke the fellow behind you in the eye with it, there is a set payment for the offence. Similarly, if you punch somebody and knock their teeth out there's a set payment for that.'

Elements of the tribal patchwork began to coalesce and harden into centres of power. Firm boundaries were established, often marked by dominant features of the landscape – features like Stonehenge. In the seventh century England became divided into seven kingdoms: Northumbria, Mercia, East Anglia, Essex, Wessex, Kent, and Sussex. Stonehenge was in Wessex. Every kingdom was further subdivided into districts called 'hundreds', each of which came under local government control. This was above all the dawn of serious dynastic kingship, and the new kings seized every means to make others submit to their territorial claims and their declared ascendancy. These were spectacularly ambitious men determined to build on every gain. 'As monarchs,' said Andrew Reynolds, 'they needed new forms through which to express their power and authority. They couldn't be everywhere at once. So the use of gallows or the display of an executed criminal was a permanent and lasting display of your authority. You may be on the other side of the kingdom, but a rotting corpse or a mouldering head stuck on a stake sent out a powerful message.'

Mike Pitts walked with Andrew Reynolds along the northern boundary of what the *Domesday Book* described as the Hundred of Swanborough. They stopped at a grassy spot where the ancient records say a gallows once stood. 'It would have been a very evocative image, I think, to people passing by,' said Andrew. 'We know, for example, that there were important routes of communication both to the north and south of here and the gallows would have been visible from all of them.'

Mike Pitts asked what the gallows would have looked like. 'You would have seen the double-post gallows, very much unlike the post-medieval single gallows in the late Anglo Saxon period. Two substantial posts were set into the ground with a beam across the top.'

'Very much like the stones at Stonehenge,' Mike observed, adding that it must have been a frightening symbol and reminder of the law's presence.

'Absolutely. Bodies were left hanging from gallows for a considerable length of time, and we often find them with the lower legs missing, with the arms missing, so presumably they'd been hanging as a form of public display for a long time. There are a number of excavated cemeteries in very similar locations to this where it would be standard to find corpses buried very shallowly just below the turf, because with criminals being at the very bottom end of the social scale, banished, outcasts, society invested the minimum amount of labour in burying them.' 'That,' said Mike Pitts, 'evoked the way in which 4-10-4 himself had been buried.'

Increasingly it looked as if the bones from the shallow grave at Stonehenge were the remains of an executed wrongdoer. At the time when Mike had believed he was investigating a killing by Romans he had called for a tooth analysis to prove the man was a Briton. That same analysis could now show if, in Anglo Saxon times, 4-10-4 had been a local man who perhaps offended against his community.

Dr Jane Evans, an isotope scientist with the British Geological Survey, showed Mike a map of the British Isles that summarized the strontium and oxygen data she referred to in order to interpret the analysis results from the tooth enamel. Red contours on the map showed the varying levels of oxygen in drinking water across Britain; in this respect the analyzed tooth had a value of minus 7.4, which placed it within a broad tract in the centre of Britain. 'However, if we look at the strontium composition of the tooth, which is going to reflect the person's diet, the water he drinks and the food he eats,' said Dr Evans, 'we can restrict his likely childhood much more closely. He had a very low value for strontium. The low values that we get in this country come predominantly from the south-east of England.'

The areas for low-level strontium were depicted as patches of yellow on the map, one patch extending upwards from the extreme south-east; the other, much smaller, lay higher up on the east coast. From the evidence of strontium deposits in the tooth, 4-10-4 could have come from either of the two yellow zones. 'If you then combine the oxygen and the strontium,' said Dr Evans, 'the only place where they overlap in Britain are in this area here.' She was pointing to the yellow patch in the south-east.

Mike said, 'That suggests quite strongly that the man is fairly local, that he comes from somewhere within south-east England or near the south coast. And, in fact, Stonehenge itself is actually inside that yellow zone.'

The probabilities had narrowed. Anyone studying the evidence was almost bound to conclude that 4-10-4 had been a local wrongdoer. But what had been his crime? What was so serious that it could have led to him being executed at Stonehenge? He lived in a period when crimes were being defined and punishments formulated for the first time in English history. The most cursory readings of seventh-century law records show that theft of property was judged to be one of the worst crimes in the calendar.

'For the vast majority of offences committed throughout the Anglo Saxon period, these could be atoned for or *were* atoned for by the payment of fines,' said Andrew Reynolds. 'In fact, capital punishment itself was very rarely enacted. The usual reason for beheading was that there was a great fear or superstition surrounding the particular individual concerned. They wanted to ensure that the beheaded person wouldn't be able to rise from the dead. So fear of the dead rising is the general explanation for beheaded individuals, but there are very few offences for which this could be undertaken.'

Decapitation *was* decreed for theft, though the punishment was reserved for theft on a large scale, cattle rustling for example, or the theft of considerable movable wealth. Probability narrowed still further and now it appeared that the remains from Stonehenge were those of a man executed for grand-scale larceny. Mike Pitts's quest was all but over. His searching had uncovered as much he could reasonably expect, although he still hankered to see what 4-10-4 had looked like.

The Stonehenge skull was badly damaged, but imagery generated by an optical surface scanner helped to rebuild the dead man's face. Robin Richards of University College Hospital, London, explained the process. 'The optical surface scanner was originally developed in order to scan patients' faces, because we wanted to monitor them before and after various sorts of facial surgery,' he said. 'It works on a very simple triangulation principle. We shine a stripe of light from a known source on to the subject and look at that stripe from an angle. By looking at it from an angle, you can see a shape profile. Knowing the geometry you can then get three-dimensional coordinates off the surface. In a typical scan, we'd get something like thirty thousand data points on the surface.'

Once the image of the Stonehenge skull had been obtained, the next step was to put a face on to it. 'The process of reconstructing the face from the skull is really separate from the scanning process. What we do is we start from the scanned skull shape and use published data, about the thickness of tissue over various parts of the surface, to extrapolate the positions that the skin surface would pass through.'

An average facial representation, made up of a number of faces, is used as the starting point for a facial appearance to map on to the skull. This face is then electronically warped until its surface matches points extrapolated from the skull.

'The process of actually warping a face onto a skull uses a relatively small number of landmark points,' Robin Richards said. 'Those thirty thousand points make the picture look the way the picture looks. Although the skull and face each have that many points, the way of mapping between the two uses a very small subset of points.'

The scanner itself can measure the object in front of it to a fraction of a millimetre, but that does not guarantee authenticity in the finished image, as Robin pointed out. 'When it comes to the reconstruction we make, there are a lot of assumptions along the way. This particular skull has been put together again from pieces and that may not have been done completely accurately. The data I work from in terms of skin thickness are typical averages and of course we can't say that this particular person had average thickness skin. So, the reconstruction that comes out at the end is an approximation of what he may have looked like. We can't say by any means that it is a spitting image.'

Mike Pitts had already accepted that much. 'In our case, what we are looking for is an impression,' he said, 'and there's going to be quite a strong element of subjectivity in certain parts of the face. For example, we've got very little in the skull that tells us what the nose looks like. The skull, of course, will never tell us what his hair looked like, his eyebrows, or the colour of his eyes. There are going to be a lot of things in the face that will be completely subjective. They are going to give us a person, but it's not a precise representation of an individual, it's a subjective one.'

What the finished reconstruction showed was an unprepossessing face, disconcerting nevertheless in its semblance of life. Here was the face of a young man; an individual electronically conjured from his ancient bones.

'Finally pinning down the death of this man has transformed the way I think about Stonehenge,' said Mike Pitts. 'From the excavations at the site there is absolutely no evidence that anything was happening there in the seventh century. So the discovery of this event, at that time, suddenly tells us that something was happening here, that people were *thinking* about Stonehenge, and that's a huge discovery.'

The collection of bones known as 4-10-4 had been the centrepiece of a demonstration of power and a public hunger to exact retribution from the guilty. It was perhaps one of authority's earliest acts of muscle flexing under a burgeoning system of law and order that survives to this day. A Wessex man but an outcast, maybe a notorious thief, was taken to a feared spot by the standing stones and there, with a minimum of delay, his judges tried him and then they executed him.

'This is somebody who had profoundly upset society and the community that knew him,' Mike Pitts said. 'He'd done something bad at a time when our very world was being shaped, our language, our law, and our landscape. He had done something to upset people and he paid for it, ending his days in the centre of what today is an icon of our indigenous past.'

Whatever the man's crime, it was considered so serious by the authorities that they sought to extend his punishment beyond the boundary of death. Barred from the new Christian burial grounds, his body was to be left to rot in the precincts of a pagan monument where, it was piously hoped, his soul would writhe in damnation for eternity.

4

THE RIDDLE
OF THE PLAGUE
SURVIVORS

IF WE VIEW THE Middle Ages in terms of disease, we can say they began with the arrival of plague at Constantinople in 542 and ended with the pandemic of bubonic plague – the Black Death – which devastated most of Europe and effectively wiped out feudalism in the mid-fourteenth century. Considered overall, the medieval period was severely unsafe for human life. For century upon century the populations of Europe and the British Isles contended with leprosy, tuberculosis, smallpox, anthrax, trachoma, scabies, erysipelas, sweating sickness and dancing mania (chorea), to cite a few, all of them diseases that attacked whole communities often in the form of an epidemic.

In England during the late thirteenth and early fourteenth century preliminary steps were taken towards fighting back: hospitals were built, quarantine was introduced to curtail the spread of infection, the burning of diseased corpses became standard practice in many regions, and legal measures were taken to limit and sometimes reverse unsanitary conditions in crowded towns and cities. Against appalling odds some progress was made, but when the Black Death (its fourteenth-century name was the Great Pestilence) swept across Europe, arriving in the southern coastal ports of England in the autumn of 1348, vigorous civic attempts to combat its spread had no effect at all.

As the infection ran its furious course sufferers were shut away in their homes and in isolation hospitals. 'The details of how plague was dealt with vary from nation to nation,' said historian Lisa Jardine, 'but the outlines of it were crude and the same, namely that a house was identified as a plague house, its inhabitants were closed in, and preventive measures were taken either with a local watch or actually posting guards to make sure that no well-meaning relatives or neighbours attempted to breach that boundary.' The period of isolation was first set at fourteen days, then it was gradually increased to forty days. Public officials in Europe introduced a system of sanitary control applicable to all contagious diseases: using observation stations, isolation hospitals, and disinfection procedures. As the Black Death tightened its grip, however, procedural niceties were slackened or abandoned; thousands of far-gone sufferers were packed together in death-houses, which were literally buildings or makeshift enclosures where people were taken to die.

Contemporary English records leave no doubt that this was the cruellest affliction the population had ever known. It was an agonizing, lethal curse from a far-off place, which no medicine could ease, let alone cure. Apart from a few seemingly miraculous instances of survival, the evidence showed that only the intervening death of the sufferer could halt the raging progress of the disease. The Benedictine monk Thomas Walsingham, in his massive *Historia Anglicana*, pondered the source of the plague: 'What foulness bore it? What darkness sent it forth?'

Bubonic plague originated in China and Inner Asia. It was eventually transmitted to Europeans when an army of Kipchaks (Mongolian people of Central Asia) laying siege to a Genoese trading post in the Crimea, catapulted plague-infected corpses into the town. The population was soon infected and the disease quickly spread from the Mediterranean ports. Lisa Jardine stressed that plague came with commerce, carried along in the directions that goods travelled. From Alexandria it crossed the Mediterranean into the great ports of Holland and Italy. In the autumn of 1347 twelve Genoese galleys sailed into the harbour at Messina in north-eastern Sicily. They carried a grotesque cargo of decaying, stinking corpses strewn across the decks. The few men still alive, riddled with plague, cried in agony. An eyewitness described the scene, 'It is impossible for the human tongue to recount the awful truth. In their bones they bore so virulent a disease that anyone who only spoke to them was seized by a mortal illness and in no manner could evade death. Those infected felt themselves penetrated by a pain through their whole bodies. It was a cruel and horrible thing...' The ships were ordered straight back out of the harbour but it was too late, the plague had arrived. Within a year it would eat the heart out of Europe.

People knew there was plague in other countries and that it was coming towards them. They either waited and prayed, sick with anticipation, or they indulged in complex, feverish rituals designed to ward off malignant spirits. There was a fourteenth-century belief that *tristesse* (sadness or melancholy) made a person more susceptible to plague, whereas happiness had a powerfully protective effect; consequently, group simulation of merriment and laughter was encouraged in some quarters. The Roman Catholic Church's position as supreme saver of souls diminished as people turned from Christianity to more esoteric or pagan doctrines to appease the oncoming blight and quieten their terrors.

'Travel stories and letters came back about this terrible cataclysmic illness that was cutting swathes through the populations of other nations and other locations,' said Lisa Jardine. 'So there was a sense in which England, for instance, actually could watch helplessly as it approached. It seemed as if there was nothing that could be done.'

In September 1348 the inevitable happened with the arrival of an infected ship at Southampton. Disease set in and soon spread to Bristol, where Henry Knighton witnessed it. 'Virtually the whole town was wiped out. It was as if sudden death had marked them down beforehand, for few lay sick for more than two or three days or even for half a day. Cruel death took just two days to burst out all over the town.'

The spread of the disease was unremitting. A French diarist, Jean Froissart, claimed that about one-third of Europe's population died in the epidemic, and that figure is nowadays accepted as fairly accurate. In England, the number of people alive in 1400 was roughly half the number of a hundred years earlier; another grim statistic is that the Black Death brought about the depopulation or disappearance of at least a thousand English villages. Historians and other researchers now accept that in Europe twenty-five million people died from the Black Death. It wasn't until the early years of the sixteenth century that Western Europe regained its pre-1348 level of population.

'I think it's really hard for us to get a grip on what it meant for something between sixty and sixty-five per cent of a locality to die,' said Jardine. 'I mean that's something on a scale that we can't conceive of. Medicine in the Middle Ages and the Renaissance was rudimentary, there were no cures for diseases, there were only attempts at warding them off, so fear of the plague was an absolute fear, if you caught it you died.'

The enormity of the entire picture – the numbers involved, the vast areas encompassed by the plague and the degree of suffering itself – is hardest of all for us to imagine. Jardine believes that one of the few ways we can grasp the scale and seriousness is to look at a fresco in the Palazzo Pubblico in Siena. It is from the middle of the fourteenth century and it depicts the city itself, showing the cathedral in the process of being built in the 1330s. 'The plague hit Siena in the 1340s,' she said. 'That cathedral stopped, they couldn't continue building. They couldn't administer the city; they couldn't deal with their dead. Everything came to a halt, and more than half and up to three-quarters of the population of plague-hit localities died.'

The catastrophe of the Black Death had countless far-reaching consequences. Wars ceased, trade slumped, but those were short-lived changes. A more lasting, more serious repercussion was the huge drop in the area of land under cultivation, because vast numbers of labourers died. This consequence alone was to be the ruin of many landowners.

Lisa Jardine expanded on this point. 'There were, if you like, two economic consequences,' she said. 'The first, dare I say it, was economic improvement for some. If you're living off the land and there are half as many of you, things get better; if you're living in a city and half the clergy die there's room for promotion. So at one level, although we don't talk about it as much, the plague actually produced economic improvement for some people. At the other end of the scale when the plague struck a locality and the entire civic structure had to be turned towards coping with disposing of the dead and dealing with quarantine and so on, and half the population had died, well, then the infrastructure just collapsed. There was nobody to collect the rubbish, nobody to make the bread, nobody to distribute food. So there's economic collapse, which incidentally regenerates surprisingly quickly. Human beings are almost outrageously resilient to epidemics. So into the space left by this collapse came, let's say, rural transients to fill the places left by those who died. And then continuing along that line, people got jobs, people got promotion and there was more food to go around, once food came back.'

Although the natural disasters of the past thousand years have been well enough recorded through their cyclic courses of calamity, economic collapse, then gradual recovery, more recent researchers have been able to uncover and illuminate patterns that were hitherto invisible. Justin Champion, a historian, has studied the death toll of the so-called Great Plague of London in 1665–66, which resulted in more than 70,000 deaths in a population estimated at 460,000. By analyzing the plague registers and cross referencing them with the burial registers he was able to establish just how many people had died from plague in each household, street by street. This research has proved to be a turning point in plague research. 'The intriguing thing is that clearly many more people contracted the disease than died,' he said. 'The images of London at a standstill, grass growing up through the cobblestones, show that there was widespread illness if not widespread mortality immediately. So we have the imponderable problem of many people contracting the disease and a high proportion of them dying, but also people who survived having experienced the disease.'

The traditional explanation had been that poverty, social status and environment all had a dramatic impact on the death toll. Champion put these assumptions to the test. 'We did that by using various computer techniques, such as relational databases linking taxation records, which gave us quite a precise description of the wealth of individual households throughout London. Then we linked those to the burial registers, so we could plot the incidences of death both in terms of social status and also in terms of space across London. So in one sense we were making maps of death.'

The results showed that the traditional explanations for survival – that poverty, overcrowding and bad hygiene tipped the scales against survival – were irrelevant. Champion was in an investigational cul-de-sac.

'Why did some people contract the disease and some not?' he asked. 'Looking at the insides of those locked-up houses, those clusterings of death, we see that people did survive that environment and I think ultimately we're forced to make the argument that it's a reflection of the different constitutions of those human individuals or those human communities.'

Here was a powerful challenge to science; what had made some people able to resist the world's deadliest disease? To understand to some extent the complexity of the challenge, it will help to take a brief look at the nature of plague. It is an infectious fever caused by the bacillus *Yersinia pestis* (named for Alexandre Yersin who, in 1894, was one of the first to describe the plague bacillus). It is transmitted by the rat flea, in particular the species *Xenopsylla cheopis*. Plague is a disease of rodents; epidemics in human beings originate when a rat flea that has already bitten an infected rat or other rodent bites a human. Once the plague bacillus has entered the bloodstream it attacks the white blood cells which are normally prominent in defending the body against infection. In humans, apart from a mild strain called ambulant plague, the infection has three forms: *bubonic*, characterized by swellings in the armpits and groins called buboes; *pneumonic*, in which areas of the lungs become infected and solidified by infected cell debris; and *septicaemic*, where the bloodstream is so heavily infested with *Yersinia* that the sufferer dies before the bubonic or pneumonic forms of the disease have time to set in.

The progress of the disease is nowadays well understood. Following initial infection, the main areas of battle between the bacilli and the body's white blood cells are bean-shaped bodies called lymph nodes in the armpits and groins. In these areas the incredibly tender and painful buboes form. When eventually the bacilli break out from the lymph nodes they disperse freely in the bloodstream and rapidly begin to multiply, moving towards wholesale colonization of the tissues. If the infected person doesn't die during the bubonic phase, recovery is possible or the disease grows more severe.

The *Yersinia* then infects the lungs and the pneumonic stage of the disease takes hold. The infection from this stage is spread from an infected individual to one who is susceptible by coughing. The symptoms of the disease appear a few days following exposure, and exposed individuals often die within two or three days of the first signs appearing. Pneumonic plague carries a very high mortality rate; almost everybody who catches it will die. More intriguingly, as Justin Champion's research showed, a few people in any given population appear to have the ability to resist the disease entirely, even though they have been heavily exposed to the lethal *Yersinia Pestis*. Dr Stephen O'Brien, a scientist and lab chief at the National Institute of Health in Washington DC, was determined to find out why.

While conducting studies of mice in the 1980s O'Brien had been struck by the ability of some of the creatures to resist a usually fatal virus infection. 'It turned out the reason for that was that the mice that didn't get the disease had a genetic resistance to it, which they handed down to their offspring,' he said. 'But the really remarkable thing was that this genetic resistance was caused by a novel gene that was stuck into the chromosomes of these animals. It was a foreshortened version of the virus itself that had gotten into an ancestor of the modern population as a sort of a natural defence against this fatal disease. When an infectious disease that causes a lot of fatality hits a population, some individuals are better equipped to defend themselves against it due to their genetic heritage. And those individuals will survive while the individuals that don't have that genetic equipment will die out.'

The conviction grew in O'Brien that there must be human genes that acted in the same way, protecting some people from diseases while others fell ill. He began a search to find the genes and over twenty years collected a huge databank of DNA from patient groups in North America. It was not an easy task. 'Although many of my colleagues who heard about our study were supportive, there were others who thought that perhaps it was a little bit too ambitious and a little bit pie in the sky. Some called it a fishing expedition because we really didn't know which gene to look at. We kept finding negative results. I think we went through over two hundred and fifty different genes without finding a thing. It was like a dry hole over and over and quite frankly I was beginning to lose my enthusiasm to discover such genes. But I was comforted at least by the fact that there are in the order of fifty thousand genes in the chromosomes of a human being, and if we'd only looked at two hundred and fifty, well, there were plenty more to look at.'

Could the survivors of the Black Death and other epidemics of plague have been protected by a gene of the kind O'Brien and his team were looking for? In order to put his theory of genetic resistance to the test Stephen O'Brien needed to find a discrete geographical area where people were known to have survived the plague, and study their descendants. 'I think all scientists like to make important discoveries,' he said, 'and like to learn new things, but I think the ones who really make the most critical advances are the ones who can't stand not understanding what happened.'

Finally O'Brien found the place he was looking for – Eyam village in Derbyshire. Eyam has a unique and extraordinary history which made it the perfect place for O'Brien to conduct a study. Hidden in the Pennines well away from the main trade routes of England, Eyam might have escaped the plague had it not been for a parcel of cloth. In September 1665, while the plague was at its height in London, the parcel, allegedly from the capital, arrived at the cottage of George Viccars, Eyam's village tailor. On arrival the cloth was damp and Viccars hung it in front of the fire to dry. He was completely unaware that the cloth was infested with fleas carrying the plague. 'In preparing to lay it out it was probably shaken,' said John Clifford, Eyam's plague historian. 'Viccars was bitten, and little red marks appeared on his hands and he didn't realize – and nobody would have told him in those days – that the red marks on his wrists were fatal and that in a short time, a very few days, he'd be dead.'

Other deaths followed and soon the villagers realized that the plague had come to Eyam. The following spring, as the weather turned warmer, the death toll began to soar. 'There was no medical help in the village,' said John Clifford, 'there was no apothecary, there was no nursing assistance, the people were totally bewildered and the only person they could really turn to was their rector and they called on him for help.'

The village rector was George Mompesson, a devout Christian and a charismatic leader. He saw at once that Eyam was doomed, but there was still the opportunity to stop the plague spreading to the neighbouring settlements. Mompesson ordered an immediate quarantine of the village. The boundaries would be sealed and nobody would be allowed in or out.

'And when they first heard this,' said Clifford, 'the shock must have been terrible, because they would realize immediately that if they accepted quarantine, cut themselves off, if they didn't die of plague they were likely to die of hunger.'

It became one of the most dramatic stories of the plague years. The nearby Chatsworth estate was the principal seat of the Earls of Devonshire, and at Chatsworth House in the spring of 1666 William Cavendish, the third Earl, appreciating the sacrifice made by the people of Eyam to minimize the risk of spreading plague in the county, arranged for food and medical supplies to be left for the villagers at a desolate spot on the southern boundary of the village, marked by a stone. People from nearby communities followed suit, and the plague-stricken villagers began leaving coins on the stone in exchange. A poignant detail is that the money was left in holes in the boundary stone, and the holes were filled with vinegar, considered a powerful disinfectant at the time, so that the infection would not be transmitted on the coins.

Soon the people of Eyam were eating better than they ever had before, knowing nevertheless, that like condemned felons enjoying their last meal, they faced certain death.

In an attempt to stem the infection within the village Mompesson decreed that the dead should be buried away from the community, up on the hillsides. Again the village followed their rector's direction even though, as John Clifford pointed out, it was for them an even greater sacrifice than quarantine itself. 'If you were not buried in God's acre with your family then on the day of judgement when all souls were gathered in, they would be absent and therefore would never be reunited with their family in paradise. So to agree to a burial in unconsecrated ground was a tremendous sacrifice.'

Joan Plant, Parish Administrator at Eyam and a descendant of survivors of the plague, is still moved by the level of self-sacrifice shown by her seventeenth-century ancestors. 'The thought of being descended from people that have done that is just something you can't even imagine. It is only as you grow up and think about things more deeply that you realize what a very special thing they did. To actually isolate themselves, knowing that they were going to die, is just beyond imagination nowadays.'

As the death toll continued to mount, the degree of personal suffering must have been immense. Every day for six days Elizabeth Hancock dragged another of her children up the hill and dug another grave. 'That was when the plague was at its height,' said John Clifford. 'It's said that the people trudging up the hill from Stoney Middleton to bring food and supplies to help the villagers looked up at the top of the hill and saw this poor woman dragging another corpse to a grave day after day.' The graves of Elizabeth's children can still be seen on the hillside. As for Elizabeth herself, in spite of having nursed and eventually buried so many of her family, she was never infected.

At the end of the summer the plague had run its course and the quarantine was lifted. Contrary to outsiders' expectations, several people appeared to have miraculously survived, and Eyam's folklore has many stories of extraordinary recovery. One tells of a man who was believed to be dead from the plague and was dragged from his bed by the village gravedigger. 'Presumably he didn't know the difference between dead and unconscious,' said Joan Plant, 'He dragged this chap down the stairs and halfway down this bloke revived and when he got to the bottom he asked for a drink. Supposedly he was OK and he survived.'

Faced with an abundance of survival tales, many of them highly colourful, local historian John Clifford took the trouble to find out if the stories amounted to more than over-embellished snippets of oral tradition, or if Eyam really did show a remarkable resistance to the onslaught of plague. 'We put it to the test. We analyzed the parish register, which starts in 1630, and we listed everybody who appeared to be alive in 1665. We deleted those who died in the plague and then we searched the register for evidence of survivors. And we went as far as 1725, which was sixty years after the plague, and we found evidence of people marrying, people having further issue, or dying, and we picked out four hundred and thirty-three survivors.'

This meant that roughly half the village had survived the plague. On the graves in Eyam churchyard today the same names recur: Blackwell, Furness, Hancock – these are the survivors. When Dr Steve O'Brien went to Eyam he found it to be a geneticist's paradise. 'The Eyam population is a fascinating opportunity to look at what is really a natural history experiment,' he said, 'to understand the interaction between plague and genetic resistance. Virtually everyone was exposed to the plague bacillus and a very high fraction of them died as a consequence. The few survivors intermarried and left a legacy, if you will, of descendants that can be typed today based upon their direct lineage tracing back to the survivors.'

Could the survivors have somehow avoided contact with the infection? It was highly unlikely. These were family units living within the confines of a small village; inevitably, everyone had made some kind of contact with sources of contamination.

As the months wore on there were more and more corpses to bury and fewer people strong and healthy enough to do the work. One man, Marshall Howe, became the self-appointed gravedigger for the village. He handled hundreds of disease-infested corpses in

Eyam, and was said to have visited virtually every house, effectively ensuring that the plague was thoroughly spread. Often, in the necessary haste to get a putrescent body under the ground, Howe would dig a grave for someone in their own garden as soon as the terrifying buboes appeared. 'He'd go to a house,' Clifford said, 'take his wheelbarrow and his pick and shovel and then dig a hole. And I tried to put myself into the minds of the people lying in bed hearing somebody digging up the garden, and knowing that they are not doing the weeding for you. It must have been a macabre feeling to hear somebody digging your grave.'

In spite of handling hundreds of infected corpses, Marshall Howe remained healthy and survived the plague. In fact, so remarkable were Eyam's recovery and survival rates that it was subsequently questioned whether plague really was the disease that hit the village. It is still sometimes suggested that the infection might have been something far less virulent. One authority has claimed that it could have been anthrax, but microbiologist Tony Hart does not agree. 'If anthrax had been transmitted on the wool that Gorge Viccars received from London he would have had to be very unlucky,' Hart said. 'The wool itself would have been prepared elsewhere, in London presumably, and made into fibres, which would then be knitted later. So most of the spores, if they had been there, would have been lost by then.'

Even if some anthrax spores had survived the long journey from London in the tailor's cloth, Hart did not believe that the disease could have infected the whole village. 'Anthrax does not pass from human to human as a rule,' he said. 'The infection passes from animal to human and that finishes it. The evidence that it was the plague is very strong. Contemporary descriptions of the disease said that it went from person to person and strongly favour the argument that it was bubonic plague rather than anthrax that affected the villagers in this case.'

John Clifford also rejected the anthrax theory. 'You find people leaving wills in which they refer to the way they wish to dispose of their livestock,' he said, 'and then if you look at the inventories, you find that they are listing considerable holdings of farm stock. If it was anthrax then the earliest victims would have been the cattle.'

Besides that, contemporary descriptions of the symptoms leave no doubt that it was plague which came to the village. So something must have protected the survivors of Eyam, and Dr Stephen O'Brien believed the answer lay in their genes. In 1996 O'Brien made a major breakthrough in his search for genes which might assist human resistance to infection; his laboratory identified the first genetic mutation that guarded against infectious disease in humans. It was named CCR5-delta 32.

'A mutation is a term geneticists use to describe a change in the DNA that is handed down from generation to generation,' O'Brien said. 'It's actually a mistake in the replication process in making sperms and eggs. Most mutations are not very good and are eliminated quickly. But occasionally one comes up that is a jewel. Sort of like if you took a hammer to the engine of a Rolls Royce a million times, one of those hammer shots would probably improve the car, the rest of them wouldn't. We believe that CCR5-delta 32 is one of those advantageous mutations.'

In the light of O'Brien's discovery, the high number of descendants still living in Eyam gave him the opportunity to put a genetic hypothesis to the test. With the villagers' co-operation he hoped to find out if CCR5-delta 32 protected their ancestors against plague in the seventeenth century.

First of all the lines of genetic descent had to be established to the satisfaction of the scientists. O'Brien met Joan Plant and other descendants of survivors at Eyam Hall, where they showed him their well-documented family trees. Remarkably, many of the family lines of descent remained intact. To O'Brien this was increasingly rich territory. 'It is simply fascinating,' said Joan Plant. 'You realize as a child, and when you are growing up, that you've got lots of aunts and uncles in the village, and you are asking your parents whose relations they are, and very often they will say, "Oh I don't know, it's perhaps your dad's second cousin." In other words it isn't really a very close relation but we are all related somehow.'

Another villager, John Hancock, is a descendant of Elizabeth Hancock, who buried her husband and six children, but survived herself. Terry Furness and Joan Plant are descended from Margaret Blackwell. Margaret was infected with plague in the spring of 1666; overcome by desperate thirst one morning, she staggered to the kitchen and drank a jug of bacon fat. Her subsequent recovery from the plague became village folklore; it was said that the bacon fat had cured her. Dr O'Brien hoped to prove otherwise.

To put the genetic hypothesis to the test, the team swabbed samples of DNA from the insides of the cheeks of a group of Eyam villagers; these specimens would be examined in the laboratory to see whether or not they contained the mutation delta 32. If the gene were not present then O'Brien would have no basis for assuming plague survivors might have been genetically protected. If the mutation *were* present, then the door would be open for an extraordinary new avenue of research. 'Eyam is a wonderful opportunity to do it,' said O'Brien, 'because like a photocopying machine their gene frequencies have been replicated for several generations without a lot of infusion from outside, so that we can look at the descendants of the bubonic plague survivors and simply question whether or not this delta 32 mutation occurs in a remarkably high frequency.'

Samples from eighty Eyam villagers were sent to University College, London (UCL) for processing. Although the CCR5 gene is present in everybody, what the UCL team was searching for was evidence of mutation – in this case a shortening of the gene – which affects the way it functions. It was potentially this short version of the gene, called delta 32, that offered protection against the plague.

O'Brien's theory was founded on the basic principle of survival of the fittest. Mutations, as he had explained, are basically genetic mistakes which crop up from time to time, and they die off unless they possess a competitive edge in the battle for survival. If a given mutation is a winner then that mutation will become more and more common in the population. 'When an infectious disease that causes a lot of fatality hits a population,' O'Brien said, 'some people are better equipped to defend against it due to their genetic heritage. And those individuals will survive, while the individuals who don't have that genetic equipment will die out.' If the survivors of Eyam had made it because of delta 32, the mutation was bound to be present in their descendants – a legacy of their ancestors' ability to encounter full-blown plague and come back alive.

When the first results came in from UCL they showed that delta 32 was present in some of the participants. That was exciting enough, but when all the results were in they showed that the mutation was present in an amazing 14 per cent of the population. Genes come in pairs, one from each parent, and the Eyam results showed some people with one copy of delta 32 and some with two copies.

O'Brien was on to something. There must have been an event at Eyam, some interference with normality, to make the gene so prevalent. If it was assumed that people who lacked the gene in 1665 were more likely to die than people who carried it, then the probability was that after the epidemic, the percentage of living people carrying the mutation would be much higher than before. But more investigation was needed, more diligent research. O'Brien found the prospect exhilarating. 'When you get a trail that you pick up you sniff at it like a bloodhound and as you get closer and closer you can almost taste the answer that's coming out,' he said. 'And when we began to unravel the secrets behind the history of delta 32, we became convinced there was an answer ready to be discovered and I really wanted to be the person that was there when we found out what happened.'

If the plague had caused the high levels of delta 32 in the people of Eyam, then Eyam would not be the only place to show such levels of the mutation. It would have been present in other parts of the world where plague had been rife, so the next step was to see how widespread it was. Working with an international team O'Brien mapped the prevalence of the mutation worldwide. They tested 4,000 volunteers in twelve different countries and the results were extraordinary. In Africa, which had remained free of plague, the mutant gene was virtually non-existent; in plague-struck Europe the gene reached staggeringly high levels, in some areas as high as 20 per cent. So, one random genetic mistake, which had occurred in just one of our European ancestors, was now being carried, in some places, by one in five of the population.

'This mutation,' O'Brien said, 'which occurred in the background of a population that we estimate was of the order of twenty thousand individuals, somehow or other went from that one mutation in twenty thousand people to about one in five in a relatively short period of time in evolutionary or genetics talk. How did this happen? Well, the only explanation that makes any sense at all is that the individuals that were carrying the mutation had a reproductive advantage.'

This could be the competitive edge that guaranteed the survival and growth of a mutation. But what gave delta 32 the edge?

'The best thing that we could think of that might be able to do that,' O'Brien said, 'was some sort of raging infectious disease outbreak, which could have killed off millions of people throughout the area where this event was taking place. But to get a little bit more specific, we wanted to see if we could actually estimate the date at which the delta 32 mutation actually occurred or, even better, the last time it was the subject of a strong selective pressure.'

O'Brien and David Goldstein, a UCL geneticist, worked over several months to pinpoint the period in history when delta 32s 'population frequency' expanded. They analyzed the DNA from O'Brien's database and were able, by looking at fractional differences between the mutations, to back-calculate the date of the original mutation using a mathematical formula. They discovered that the gene's frequency increased dramatically in the northern European population approximately 700 years ago. 'I knew it was medieval times,' said O'Brien, 'but I'm no historian, so I really did have to go and try to look up what was going on seven hundred years ago, and I was struck by the candidate that jumped out at me, which, of course, was the Black Death.'

This was another compelling support for O'Brien's theory. At the very time when plague exploded in Europe, the delta 32 mutation expanded in the population. If O'Brien was right he would have found the answer to one of the toughest historical mysteries ever, namely the riddle of why some people miraculously escaped the plague.

In the fourteenth century, the mystery gave rise to numerous theories, many of them complex and centring on the disposition of the heavens at the time of a person's birth. Conflicting schools of medical thought proposed all kinds of preventatives, if not cures; it was commonly believed that people who adhered firmly to a preventative regime, for example regular doses of treacle in hot wine (not treacle as we know it today, however), reinforced by pledgets of gin-soaked cotton in the nostrils, would most likely ward off the infection. Countless expensive and often painful treatments and talismans were marketed by quacks who preyed on the terrors of a vulnerable population. For many, as despair overtook them, there was no plausible conclusion other than that God had chosen to slay the many and spare only a few, for reasons best known to Himself. 'It was when plague had struck in a district,' Lisa Jardine said, 'that people asked themselves whether they had been especially wicked, and if they were then spared then why had they been spared? Well, it was God's will that they had been spared.'

In his researches John Clifford detected something similar. 'There was a belief that the nice people, the rich people, the quality families, would be immune from plague, as would the clergy. But of course we know that the plague was rife in monastic establishments in Europe and many monasteries were almost totally wiped out, faith or no faith. The plague didn't take much notice of that.'

Plague in Europe and the British Isles was to recur in sporadic bursts over the next 300 years. Then, at the end of the seventeenth century, it disappeared. Why was that? Could it have been the increasing penetration of delta 32? Certainly the gradual decline in the death rate showed that plague no longer had the devastating effect on communities that it had when it first arrived. 'The first time a plague hit a community was always the worst,' said Jardine. 'In 1348 the plague came into England – it was cataclysmic. It was never that bad again. For a historian looking at the way second strikes of the plague seemed to have less impact on local communities, I suppose from a modern point of view it looks like some kind of immunity was built up.'

The evidence was accumulating: this tiny genetic mistake, delta 32, could have been protecting generations of families from the plague, ensuring their survival while others around them died. But what was the precise nature of this gift the early survivors bequeathed their descendants? Could it confer immunity from other deadly diseases?

If we look more closely at the mechanism of plague infestation, a fascinating coincidence shows up. As soon as the plague bacilli enter the body, the immune system tries to fend them off by surrounding them with white blood cells, which are capable – in less virulent infections – of 'swallowing' invading pathogens (the process is called phagocytism) and destroying them by a process of intracellular digestion. But plague is able to trick the immune system. It attaches itself to a subset of the white blood cells, known as the macrophages, and instead of being attacked by them it renders them ineffective. It is carried by the macrophages to the lymph nodes in the groin and armpits where it replicates swiftly, causing the terrible buboes that typify the infection. Another disease known to play that devastating trick on the immune system is AIDS.

Justin Champion, whose 'death maps' helped nullify the traditional explanations for plague survival, found it a bizarre experience to study the cultural impact of the plague on the late seventeenth century, while being able to read in the newspapers about the spread of AIDS that was threatening our own culture. 'The medical connections are obviously difficult for me to make as a historian,' he said, 'but the cultural responses are almost identical. The scapegoating of particular groups – the poor, the ungodly, the sexually deviant – is clearly the sort of reaction that a community under stress faces. The attempt to segregate, lock up, hide, deny that there is a particular part of the community that's suffering, is again something we see in both the twentieth century and in the seventeenth century. The very language – we already talk about a gay plague – makes the same point. We talk about something that is silent and secret and insidious and dangerous and subversive and unknown. And I think it is fear that drives both of those sorts of popular narratives.'

As happened with the Black Death in the fourteenth century, the mysterious new disease (one of its early names was Gay Compromise Syndrome) caught everyone off guard. Don Kotler was a young American doctor specializing in gastro-intestinal disorders at the time AIDS, an acronym of Acquired Immune Deficiency Syndrome, began its catastrophic spread. 'It was the summer of 1981,' he said. 'It was, in some ways, a different time in medicine. Through the 1960s and 1970s medicine had become very arrogant and very cocky. Transplantation had become a real phenomenon and a real option for people. There were advances in my speciality, gastro-enterology, in cardiology, nephrology, renal disease with dialysis... it had left a feeling that medicine could do anything. So we were a pretty arrogant lot of people. And then, probably starting in the late 1970s, but for me in mid-1981, we began to see people who were ill in a way that was resistant to our therapy. It was a humbling experience.'

For a practising physician it seemed that the terrain and nature of disease were shifting. And there was a distinct sense of emergency. 'It was a siege,' he said. 'A day wouldn't go by in which there wouldn't be some unexpected complication. There was no time to think, it was all a matter of reacting, much, I guess, like one would react in a war, during an attack. It was a siege mentality.'

AIDS, like the Black Death, was attacking the immune system, the very bodily system designed to fight off invasion by infectious organisms. 'What was so bewildering was that the rules of medicine had changed,' Kotler went on. 'Normally when patients presented a series of complaints, there was a single diagnosis that would explain the complaints. If someone had fever and anaemia and other symptoms, we could find a single disease that would explain every one of those complaints. It's the so-called law of parsimony, or Occam's razor. In fact, when we saw AIDS patients for the first time what we found were multiple causes for the same complaint, not a single cause for pneumonia, but three different organisms all causing pneumonia at the same time. It's much like defending a farm. You could defend against the predator, the fox. That wasn't the problem, that was what we had always done in medicine, look for the pathogen or look for the fox. What we had suddenly was more similar to a barn door being open, and anything could walk in and anything could walk out. It was as though these patients were suddenly exposed to numerous diseases, not a single one.'

If doctors sensed urgency, however, they did not sense the enormity of the syndrome confronting them. 'I must say that the original response of the medical community was not panic,' Kotler said, 'and the original response in society was not panic. It was more that the problems were ignored. There was a lack of panic. There was a lack of realizing that not only was this something new but that it was something profound. What we saw, those of us who were taking care of patients, was a logarithmic growth. We saw one, then we saw two, then we saw eight, then we saw sixteen, the numbers rising very, very strongly and yet the hospitals, and society in general, really did not respond for several years. The danger was really discounted. In fact for those of us taking care of patients, it was like watching an accident or a tragedy occurring in slow motion, realizing that every time a choice came up to do something that would help stop the spread of the disease, society tended to do the wrong thing. That's really a problem that's continued even to now. Just as an example, some time in mid- to late 1983, it became clear that intravenous drug use was a risk factor for HIV and for a period of six to nine months there was a huge increase in the number of people who presented looking for detox to get off drugs, or methadone maintenance to try to stay away from using needles. In fact, society did not respond at all in terms of increasing the number of spots for people to get methadone. There were arguments after arguments which continue today about needle exchange and changing risk through behavioural change. It's a problem that's continued in all the other countries. If it happened in the United States and France and Britain and Australia first, it then went through the rest of Europe, then South America and then Asia and Africa. Even until this summer [2000] when inexplicably, the president of South Africa decided to question whether HIV even was the cause of AIDS and used that as an excuse not to provide counselling or indeed any kind of resources to try to stop the spread of the disease.'

AIDS is probably the most serious and daunting disease in the history of humanity. Like all profound malignancies it begins without sound or sensation, and it bides its time. Mirroring the behaviour of the plague bacillus, the HIV (human immunodeficiency virus) disrupts the immune system, and by an almost identical means. HIV is a retrovirus, which means that unlike other living organisms it contains the genetic material RNA (ribonucleic acid) instead of the usual DNA (deoxyribonucleic acid); to multiply, a retrovirus employs a special enzyme to convert its RNA to DNA, which will then integrate with the DNA of the host. When HIV enters the body, the immune system alerts white blood cells which engulf the invading pathogen. But the HIV, like *Yersinia pestis*, targets the cells and instead of being destroyed by them it renders them ineffective. This leaves the unwitting host open to a variety of infections, neurological diseases and malignancies. Meanwhile, like the plague bacillus, the HIV colonizes its victim's body.

For Stephen O'Brien, the mechanism of HIV infection raised fascinating implications for his theory about plague. 'There are toxins produced by the chromosomes of the plague bacteria that target precisely the same cells that HIV enters. The connections are indirect, but it's like finding two very, *very* similar kinds of murders occurring in a very small town in Pennsylvania at the same time, and us wondering whether or not the same person committed them.'

The 'murder mystery' might have remained unsolved had it not been for a man called Steve Crohn. In the 1970s Crohn was living in San Francisco with his lover, Jerry. Before the spectre of AIDS appeared, Crohn had a freewheeling lifestyle that included a good deal of homosexual activity. 'There were more gay people; there were more *people*,' said Crohn, 'because it was the baby-boom generation and we had more of an opportunity to express ourselves. Part of that was very much a sexual expression so in that sense it was hedonistic. We had music, we had disco, we had drugs, and we could dance all night and fuck all day. I think the liberation was the most important part of that, not the sexuality... A lot of other people were enjoying being on the dance floor, it was as much an important political factor – feeling free – as it was being able to have a variety of partners.'

But in 1982 signs of a new disease began to appear, a lethal infection that apparently targeted homosexual men. It threw the gay community into turmoil. Steve Crohn looked on as one by one his friends began to sicken from the baffling ailment. One of them was his lover, Jerry. 'It was the same as any plague or any scourge,' Crohn said, 'there was absolutely no name for it and yet you were living in a very modern society with supposedly state-of-the-art medical techniques... It was extremely frustrating. It was shocking and it was scary and you didn't know what it was, so there was a mystery of suddenly this person went from being thirty-four years old and totally vital, and a gymnast and handsome and healthy and he ate well, exercised well, and then was suddenly like an eighty-five-year-old man.'

Faced with the inevitable, Crohn tried nevertheless to maintain a hopeful outlook. But it was hard. 'On a day-to-day basis you know you're losing the person that you're in love with. They're going into some other kind of state, mentally, emotionally, physically, and there's no name for it, so you really don't know what the outcome is. You just keep maintaining this positive picture of them as a healthy person until you finally turn a corner and to be honest it was an astrologer that told me that he was going to die, it was never a doctor.'

Doctors have their own sad recollections of encountering young men suffering from AIDS, and having to break the news to their families. 'A recurring memory is not that I had to tell the parents that their son had AIDS,' said Don Kotler, 'but that I first had to tell their parents that their son was gay. The mothers all seemed to know. The fathers seemed not to have realized. The mothers, in general, discounted the fact; the fathers had much more trouble dealing with the fact that they had a gay son. And I must say, interestingly enough, afterwards, and I kept in contact with a number of the parents, the mothers seemed to weather the experience much better than the fathers. Near the end the fathers would realize that a son is a son no matter what, and then have a lot of difficulty adjusting once the son had died.'

When Steve Crohn's lover Jerry died on 4 March 1982, it was the beginning of a long trek through grief as one by one other friends began to die. 'You can't really process that many people dying all the time,' he said. 'Over the course of that decade I lost about seventy to eighty people. So you're talking about a lot of funerals, a lot of memorials... and there was really nobody left.'

Nobody, that is, except Steve Crohn.

'We always identified it as like being at war, because the only other experience you could find where all of your friends of the same age were dying around you would be if you were in the war and your platoon was wiped out. The thought was that I would eventually get AIDS and die...'

By 1985 7,000 Americans had been diagnosed as having AIDS. As it was with plague, victims of AIDS suffered doubly by being condemned to a grisly death and being rejected by society. Gays were blamed for the disease and were demonized. Curiously, throughout the carnage that took away practically all his friends, Crohn himself did not succumb. Test after test confirmed that he was HIV negative. 'I was mentioning this question... to a family relative at some party and they said, "Well, why don't they test you, then?" And I thought, gee, that makes sense, why aren't they studying me? So that just sort of inspired me to make another round of phone calls to doctors and see if there were any trials out there, and there weren't. I really did a lot of phone work, there weren't any trials, there was nobody studying HIV-negative men, until I found Bill Paxton.'

A young man determined to make his mark on the AIDS story, Bill Paxton persuaded his laboratory chief at the Aaron Diamond AIDS Research Center in New York to let him try a novel experiment. The idea was to work on the blood cells of men and women who were at very high risk of HIV infection, but who had not been infected, to try to find clues about how the virus worked. 'At the time the centre had no study of people who were exposed to HIV but who had remained negative,' Paxton said. 'There were studies of long term non-progressors, rapid progressors, acute serial converters, all those groups were being studied, but at that point there was no specific study on exposed uninfected groups. And being in New York you knew those people were there – I mean, you *met* those people.'

Paxton's working method was dramatically direct. He took samples of white blood cells from the high-risk uninfected group and exposed them, in the test tube, to a massive bombardment of HIV virus – the dose was 3,000 times the normal amount of HIV necessary to infect a cell. In the case of Steve Crohn's cell sample an amazing thing happened. In spite of the overkill dosage of HIV, the cells remained uninfected.

In the laboratory Paxton showed the clear comparative evidence of Crohn's sample alongside others tested at the same time. 'The red colour in the well indicates the amount of viral activity. As you go across here these individuals have lots of P24 antigen, or viral reproduction, and then you come to Steve's white blood cells and you see there is no viral reproduction whatsoever from these cells. These all stay white, suggesting no viral replication.'

At first Paxton thought he had made a mistake. 'We thought maybe we had infected the culture with bacteria or whatever, so we went back to Steve. But again it was the same result. We went back again and again. Same result.'

This was clinical paradox on a grand scale. The HIV virus can only multiply inside the blood cells, and in Crohn's case no penetration of the cells was occurring. After some deliberation Paxton's team decided to run a check on Crohn's DNA to try to discover what was stopping the HIV virus from penetrating his cells.

Like plague, HIV targets macrophages, though in the case of the virus the targeted cell type is the T-cell, a larger version of the ordinary white blood cell. In order to enter this cell the HIV virus has to use a gateway provided by a gene called CCR5, which manufactures a receptor – the chemical equivalent of a docking station for the virus. Once HIV has docked to the CCR5 receptor the cell's gateway is open. But Steve's genes were different. His CCR5 gene had no receptor for HIV to dock on to. The virus, therefore, was unable to enter his cells.

'The CCR5 protein is defective,' Bill Paxton explained. 'So when the gene makes it, the protein can't get to the surface of the cells. Therefore, the virus can't use it to gain entry. It's like a block. The cell is missing the lock that's required for it to get in. It's got the key but there is no lock.'

Crohn's CCR5 gene produced faulty protein because it had a segment missing, a situation known in genetic terminology as a deletion, which was then identified as CCR5-delta 32. This was, of course, the very entity Stephen O'Brien and his team had uncovered in 1996 as they searched for genes that might assist human resistance to infection.

'The news was very soberly presented to me and I took it in a very cautious manner,' said Steve Crohn. 'But the results were very exciting, to be able to tell my family I may never be able to catch AIDS, that was like the first reaction, I think... Really to tell my nieces and nephews and my sisters that they would not have to go through what I saw some other families go through, I think that was the greatest bonus.'

Stephen O'Brien was quick to pick up the baton. Analyzing the data from thousands of patients whose blood he had been collecting for years, he was able to screen all of them for delta 32, then compare that to their clinical picture with regard to HIV. He found a direct correlation: the people who had succumbed to AIDS all had normal functioning CCR5 genes. But a high proportion of the patients who had remained healthy in spite of being at high risk from HIV, carried delta 32. The case was proven: delta 32 conferred a powerful resistance to HIV.

'The explanation was really quite simple,' said O'Brien. 'These people did not have the entry portal for HIV, and therefore even if they were exposed over and over they did not become infected. And this was the first genetic restriction that had been discovered against an infectious disease in humans. And it was a whopper.'

Could the plague use the same lock-and-key mechanism to penetrate a cell? The knowledge that delta 32 did indeed confer resistance to AIDS, a disease remarkably similar to the plague in the way it deceived the immune system, hinted that an answer might be tantalizingly close.

Steve Crohn carried two copies of the delta 32 mutation, one inherited from each parent, and that made him completely immune to infection by HIV. But what about people with only one copy? 'Even among people that did become infected there were differences that were unexplained,' said O'Brien. 'Some people got sick and died of AIDS within a few years of getting infected. For most it was about ten years before they became infected. But there was a small fraction of people that survived AIDS for twenty years or longer without having any symptoms whatsoever, in spite of the fact that they were infected with HIV.'

O'Brien had discovered the answer to something which had puzzled AIDS researchers for two decades. People with one copy of the delta 32 mutation took much longer to develop the disease. They had a *partial* resistance.

The Eyam mystery was finally unravelling. Some of the population had died quickly from plague, some fell sick and then miraculously recovered, others were never sick at all. Now for the first time there was a biological explanation. 'I think it's plausible,' said O'Brien, 'that having the different genome type with respect to a resistance gene such as delta 32 may explain some of the differences that the survivors in Eyam have had.'

Elizabeth Hancock had nursed her husband and six of her children through the ravages of plague yet she herself had completely resisted the disease. Could her extraordinary resistance have meant that she, like Steve Crohn, carried two copies of delta 32?

Margaret Blackwell actually contracted plague, but she recovered. Old wives' tales about the virtues of bacon fat aside, could it have been that a single copy of delta 32 enabled

Margaret to survive long enough to throw off the disease? 'If the individual who has two copies of the normal gene got sick and died in five days,' said O'Brien, 'it may be that individuals with one copy of the normal gene and one copy of delta 32 actually postpone the onset of death for twelve days. In the meantime the armament of the immune system, which has many different battalions, if you will, could be mounting an immune response sufficient to clear out the bacterium so that the individual actually survives rather than dies.'

The traditional story of Eyam now has a new twist. Far from being the indomitable killer it was once thought to be, the plague actually met strong resistance in many of the individuals it attacked. This resistance could not be induced by piety, apothecaries or good breeding. It was a *genetic* difference that has been handed down to many of us, a legacy of our ancestors' ability to survive the plague. It is an inheritance which continues to protect against other deadly infections. The riddle of the plague survivors appears to have been solved, and science has filled in a few more of history's blanks.

5

THE REAL
ZULU DAWN

HISTORY MAKES IT ABUNDANTLY clear that the native peoples of Africa were treated monstrously by the colonizing whites, and in retrospect it is small wonder. The racism that infested British culture in the nineteenth century allowed little room for the notion that dark-skinned peoples were real human beings, let alone sentient individuals with traditions, cultural values, and the right to be respected. Much of the bigotry implanted in young Victorian heads by their elders – and teachers among them – was founded on the belief that the brown- and black-skinned races of the earth were naturally inferior to those of a lighter tint.

Prominent among scholars who advanced the myths of racial and class superiority was Sir Francis Galton, an English anthropologist revered in his time for his studies of human intelligence. Nowadays Galton is remembered for his pioneering work on the science of eugenics, a name he coined and which meant, his journal tells us, 'the investigation of the conditions under which men of a high type are produced'. Galton believed that by applying the principles of selective breeding to the pairing of males and females – for centuries a practice common in the raising of livestock – the human race could be immeasurably improved. This eugenic principle was echoed in the work of the German philosopher Friedrich Nietzsche, who proposed a form of genetic selection to create a new and powerful race of people who would dominate their natural inferiors, just as in nature man naturally dominates the animals. In the twentieth century the Nazi belief in Aryan superiority and the innate inferiority of Jews owed much to the contributions of Adolf Hitler, who always acknowledged his debt to Nietzsche.

In nineteenth-century Britain the work of Sir Francis Galton was disseminated by his supporters in schools and through the pages of influential journals, which helped establish the conviction that the wealth and superiority of the British social élite was the result of breeding from superior stock. Careful selection was everything. In his book *Hereditary Genius* Galton wrote, 'It would be quite practical to produce a highly gifted race of men by judicious marriages during several consecutive generations.'

Fifty-six years after *Hereditary Genius* was published, an outpost of Galton's movement in the United States, calling itself the American Eugenics Society, was openly proclaiming the superiority of the white race over other races, adding that Nordic whites were most superior of all. If racial attitudes prevailing in Galton's Victorian England were not so extreme, they nevertheless embodied certain inflexible principles, for example, racial inferiority equals weakness, and for the enrichment of civilization, the strong *must* manipulate the weak. Nowhere was that belief more keenly cherished than amongst the colonizers of British political life; and nowhere was it more savagely enacted than in southern Africa in the 1870s, as the forces of white colonial expansion smashed their way across the Zulu homeland.

Some understanding of how the Zulus grew to power helps us understand the British military leaders' determination to decimate them. The founder of the Zulu Empire in southern Africa was the renowned chief Shaka who, at the peak of his powers, created a disciplined, supremely powerful nation whose principles survive in the culture of present-day Zulus.

Shaka was born in 1787, the son of Senzangakona, chieftain of the Zulu, and his wife Nandi. Shaka was six years old when Senzangakona and Nandi separated. Nandi took her son back to her home clan, the Langeni, where Shaka spent a boyhood with no father, living like an outcast among people who shunned his mother because she had flouted marital tradition.

After nine years of alienation and intermittent friction, Nandi and Shaka were thrown out by the Langeni. Following a term of homelessness, the Dletsheni, a subclan of the powerful Mtetwa, took them in. When Shaka turned twenty-three the chief of the Mtetwa enlisted him for military service, and for six years Shaka served as a distinguished warrior of the Mtetwa Empire.

When Shaka's father died in 1816 the Mtetwa chief released Shaka from the army and appointed him to take charge of the Zulus. At that time they numbered fewer than 2,000, being among the smallest of the 800 Eastern Nguni-Bantu clans. From the day Shaka took control, the Zulus' rise to power began. His rule was harsh and inflexible from the outset. He would tolerate no opposition and dispensed instant death to anyone who argued with him. A formerly loose-knit, undisciplined clan began to shape into an organized body with a sense of direction. The Zulus may have begun to live with a measure of fear, but they also began to demonstrate a steady growth in their stature as human beings.

Shaka's major act as leader was to restyle the army. The Zulus, like all the other clans, carried ox-hide shields and slender-shafted throwing spears. Battles until then had been short and fairly bloodless affairs, where the side that realized it was losing would make a strategic withdrawal before they suffered too many casualties. Shaka changed all that. He armed his men with short-handled, long-bladed assegais, designed for stabbing. These weapons, fashioned originally by the Berbers and taken up by the Moors, were efficient and lethal, but they required the Zulu to learn to fight at close quarters. Next, Shaka inaugurated a regimental system based on age groups. Each regiment was billeted at a separate village, and was distinguishable by its own shield markings, headdresses, and ornaments. Shaka devised a standard tactical manoeuvre, which the Zulu used in every battle they fought; it went as follows. The regiments involved (known by the collective term *impi*) formed themselves into four groups. The strongest, called the 'chest,' closed in on the enemy from a frontal position and began to pin them down. Meanwhile two 'horns' of soldiers ran out from behind the chest on either side, encircling the enemy and attacking them from behind. The reserve unit of the manoeuvre, the 'loins', sat nearby with their backs to the battle; this was to keep them from becoming overexcited and therefore less in control of themselves. They could be summoned by hand signals from the *indunas* (officers), to reinforce any part of the ring of warriors if the enemy showed signs of breaking loose.

Myth has it that a regiment could regularly march 50 miles a day, sustaining themselves with cereals and cattle commandeered from villages along the way. Boys, who had the job of carrying the warriors' cooking pots and sleeping mats, assisted speed of movement. In an impressively short space of time, the Zulus became the most effective and most feared body of tribal fighting men ever encountered in southern Africa.

Shaka was not a negotiator at any stage of his career. He fought for extinction, and any remaining members of the clans he defeated were absorbed and became his own people. It took the Zulus and their army less than a year to quadruple their numbers. In 1817 the Mtetwa chief, who until then had remained Shaka's overlord, was murdered. His death meant there was no further barrier to Zulu expansion. In the following two years Shaka destroyed the Qwabe and the Ndwandwe, the two clans big enough to pose any threat to the Zulus. There followed a series of four annual campaigns during which the Zulus wiped out the intricate plexus of clan domains south of the Zulus' territories.

In 1824 the first Europeans arrived in Port Natal, which is now Durban. Settlers of the Farewell Trading Company, twelve in all, erected a post on the hill-enclosed bay and within a few days they confronted Shaka, whose village, Bulawayo, just over a hundred miles north of Port Natal. One of the settlers, Henry Francis Fynn, who later became a fluent speaker of Zulu, recorded in his journal that Shaka appeared to be fascinated by their mannerisms, their way of life and the gifts they brought. But Shaka made it clear that he believed his own culture was much superior to that of the Europeans.

In 1827 Shaka's mother Nandi died, and the effect on Shaka was catastrophic. His grief was huge and so was his anger, an unreasoning rage that resulted in the banning of crop planting and the indiscriminate killing of 7,000 Zulus; pregnant women were put to death along with their husbands, while farm animals in their thousands were slaughtered. Early the following year Shaka despatched regiments to the south in an all-out raiding sortie that took them clear to the borders of the Cape Colony. As soon as the men returned, exhausted and counting on the customary three months' rest, Shaka sent them on a raiding mission many miles away to the north. For those close to the demented Shaka this was the last straw. In September 1828 two of his half-brothers, Dingane and Mhlangana, murdered him. Shaka died a heartless, deranged tyrant with his faculties in chaos. But his legacy endured. He was the creator of a uniquely powerful empire, headed by men of iron discipline and legendary ferocity. Because of Shaka, the name Zulu was feared and respected in Africa as none had ever been before.

By the time Queen Victoria's empire reached its peak, Britain had colonized a quarter of the world's land. And on the eastern seaboard of southern Africa in the 1870s the British

Army spearheaded the growth of Empire with unrelenting force, all the time keeping an eye on the Zulus. For fifty years the region had seen steady penetration by white missionaries and traders, yet the Zulus maintained their supremacy in the region, creating a daunting barrier to large-scale colonization. The British, feeling their own strength, decided the situation was intolerable. The authority of the Zulu tribe must be broken, and who better to do that than a body of British fighting men, armed with the very latest weaponry?

'I think it's very much part of the Victorian mindset generally, that independent kingdoms needed to be put in their place, they needed to realize who was boss,' said Ian Knight, a prominent Anglo–Zulu war historian. 'British prestige, British power was dependent on the whole idea of being able to defeat and suppress anybody who objected to British rule. The Zulus had come to be seen as a symbol of resistance, a symbol of the resistance of indigenous African peoples to British rule in southern Africa.'

Sir Henry Bartle Frere, the British High Commissioner, presented an aggressive ultimatum to the Zulu king, Cetshwayo, demanding that he and his nation peacefully submit to the will of the colonizing emissaries in the form of Lord Chelmsford, KCB, the Lieutenant General commanding the British Forces in southern Africa. The thinking behind the ultimatum was that King Cetshwayo would not dream of obeying it, and his refusal would provoke a war. At the same time this would allow the British to claim they had acted in a proper diplomatic manner. They could say that they had had legitimate complaints with King Cetshwayo, and that the king, being a ruthless despot, had not listened to them – had not, in fact, paid the slightest attention to their advice for living peacefully alongside the colonizers. 'The whole idea,' said Ian Knight, 'was that Lord Chelmsford would bring his armies in and Britain would be able to go to war. The assumption was that within a couple of weeks they would defeat the Zulu kingdom and could get on with sorting out the rest of southern Africa.'

Knight believes there was imperial over-confidence in Lord Chelmsford's belief that he could quickly win a war with the Zulus. It was true that he had brought a speedy conclusion to a messy little war on the Cape frontier six months before Bartle Frere's ultimatum, and that might have helped bolster the self-confidence of Chelmsford and his aides. 'At one stage,' Knight said, 'somebody on Chelmsford's staff remarked in a rather blasé manner that with a company and a half of redcoats, you could march through the length and breadth of Zululand. There was a feeling that there was nothing the Zulus could do that was ever going to stop even the smallest numbers of trained British troops. But the whole history of the Zulus was that they had a military tradition going way back to King Shaka's time, and there was nothing to suggest they were going to be a walkover.'

But in the upper levels of military decision-making, precautionary judgement was regularly dismissed as defeatist claptrap. Wariness did not chime with colonizing ambition; the British were the masters of the world and could therefore do practically anything they wanted. Amplifying the need to subjugate the Zulus were the demands of the white settlers to the south of Zululand, who were frightened of their neighbours and wanted them brought under control. 'So there they were, as far as the colonists were concerned, little white islands in a great black sea,' said Professor John Laband, a historian from the University of Natal. 'All you needed were Zulus to come over the river and that would be the end of you. There was that great fear of what they might do.'

There was also a deeper, more neurotic anxiety about a likely backlash from the black people of Africa in general. 'Most whites in southern Africa demonized the Africans,' said John Laband, 'because of the fear they had of what they might do. And for the colonists in Natal they were, after all, next door to the largest independent African state still in southern Africa [Zululand] and one, moreover, which was particularly militaristic in their eyes. So the popular image of the Zulus was that they were ready to rampage and attack, that there was a great sort of man-slaying war machine that would be unleashed at any moment. But in the wider sense of things there was also a feeling that the Zulus and their King were at the head of a black conspiracy in Southern Africa. There was certainly a feeling that somehow all the Africans in southern Africa were going to be co-ordinated into some great uprising against white rule.'

In the wider context, it must be remembered that though the centre of the British sphere of colonial interest at the time was India, there was a clear element of confederation in British foreign policy. It was important to ensure that the colonies paid for themselves. All in all, the suppression of the Zulu empire appeared to make good colonial sense. Over and above the fear of what the warriors might do to the colonists, Professor Laband detected a powerful element of territorial greed behind the pressure to have something done about these tribal irritants. 'There was Zululand itself, all this land, especially along the coast. If someone was thinking of growing sugar cane, coffee, indigo, or whatever else, there was all this coastal land to move into.'

There was, too, the thorny fact that Zululand lay across the path to the north; if a settler was thinking of extending his commercial interests in that direction, Zululand stood in the way. Suppression of the Zulu, moreover, would create a vast and very cheap labour force. 'This was a time in southern Africa when the mineral revolution was starting,' Laband said. 'Commercial farming was starting, too. It was a time when labour was required.'

So a war with the Zulus was engineered, and while the British Army eventually emerged victorious, the battles fought during the campaign included the worst defeat inflicted on it during the entire Victorian era. On 22 January 1879, at the British Army encampment at Isandlwana in Zululand, 850 white troops and 470 of their black allies, known as the Natal Native Contingent, were killed. The first battalion of the 24th Infantry Regiment was almost entirely wiped out, apart from a single company which was engaged elsewhere at the time. 'All of the officers who held field command, except one, were killed,' said Ian Knight. 'Nobody who fought on foot in this battle actually got away at all. It was extremely apocalyptic in terms of the casualty roll. The camp was wiped out and hardly anybody lived to tell the tale. Only the shattered remnants of the battalion, exhausted and traumatized, managed to get away, and that was all that was left of an invading army.'

It is ironic therefore that Isandlwana would prove to be the undoing of the Zulus. The British could not tolerate such a loss and so reinforcements were sent, in their thousands, to crush the Zulus once and for all. But until recently, the underlying causes of such a resounding British defeat have remained obscure.

On the day of the battle Lord Chelmsford left the camp at Isandlwana early, before dawn, and it was not until after dark that he and his small army returned. His men were exhausted from marching all day in the hills of Zululand; to top all that and the horror of what they encountered on their return, Chelmsford decided that they should remain at the camp overnight. His men could scarcely believe it. 'The battlefield was carpeted in dead men and dead animals,' said Ian Knight. 'Somebody said that they couldn't put a foot a yard in any direction without stepping over a dead body. Most of the British bodies had been stripped and disembowelled by the Zulus. People lay down to sleep, waking up in the morning to find that they had been lying next to corpses. A soldier recalled that he tripped over something, and as he fell he put his hands out in front of him, and the hands fetched up inside the belly of a disembowelled corpse. They had the most ghastly night, which stretched their nerves almost to breaking point.'

Though a terrible defeat for the British Army, indeed an exceptional one, the battle of Isandlwana has never been prominent in the popular history books. Later, on the same day as that momentous battle, a handful of British soldiers success-fully defended the garrison at Rorke's Drift, 10 miles west of Isandlwana, against 4,000 Zulus. The military élite immediately leapt at the chance to mask the humiliation of their earlier defeat. Rorke's Drift was inflated out of all proportion and became a famous victory. Of the 300 Victoria Crosses that have ever been awarded, eleven were for bravery at Rorke's Drift. In 1963 the story of the event was immortalized for successive generations in Cy Endfield's celebrated motion picture *Zulu*, which made a star of Michael Caine. Yet, as Ian Knight has pointed out, what happened at Rorke's Drift was a sideshow compared to the battle of Isandlwana. 'Rorke's Drift was just a piece of good news at the end of a very bad day,' he said. 'It's actually well known in historical circles, certainly in the UK, that the two most popular battles in nineteenth-century British military history are the Battle of Waterloo and Rorke's Drift. Now Waterloo obviously was an immensely important battle in terms of European history, it was dramatic, it featured colourful characters in Wellington and Napoleon and it changed the course of Europe thereafter. Rorke's Drift was an extremely insignificant action, if you look at it in those terms, but it has a similar kind of, dare I say, *glamour* and colour and drama and heroism to it that really captures something in the popular imagination.' Knight does not deny that bravery and valour were displayed in the skirmish, but he sees an element of inevitability in the event. 'Where were the British going to go? No doubt there were some great tales of bravery at Rorke's Drift but at the end of the day they were pinned down – they had no option but to stand and fight. As they discovered at Isandlwana, they would have all been cut down if they had run.'

Contrary to popular misinformation, the Zulus were not warmongers, although they were good at war if driven to it. Their society was organized into regiments, but by the 1870s these were used for hunting and for policing the villages. There had been no war with whites since 1838, and since 1815 they had not fought with any other tribe. To the spiritual elders of the Zulu nation, the perpetuated warlike image is insulting. Credo Mutwa, a Zulu *sanussi* (or high medicine man) explains. 'The image that has been projected by historians of the Zulu people is that of raging, snarling, bloodthirsty savages, out to massacre their enemies. No, no. First of all, let me explain that to the Zulu people warriors were not just weapon-carrying monsters who were out to slaughter people like gods. A warrior was a mystic. A warrior was a philosopher. I was trained, as a young child of fourteen years, in the ways of the ancient warriors. One of the things that the old men who trained us, me and the other boys, said was that you must respect your enemy. You must admire and love your enemy.'

The reasoning, Credo explained, was that when a warrior was fighting in the bush, it was a deadly game of hide-and-seek among the trees. The warrior did not know where his enemy was or what surprise he might spring. A warrior who allowed himself to be blinded by hatred of his adversary was only multiplying his own difficulties. 'You must project such love, such admiration towards your enemy, that you will be able to sense exactly where he is. Even when you are hand-to-hand, spear-to-spear with your enemy, it must be with admiration and respect.'

And if his people were inherently warlike, Credo asked, why did they call war by a word which has the same root as their word for evil? In the language of the Zulus, war was known as *impi*, and the word for evil, any evil, is the same. 'If I say this is an evil thing, in the language of the Zulus, I say the word "*impi*".

Our people also called an army by the same name by which they called war, "*impi*". So our word for army and war was the same, and it meant that which is evil.'

The fact that the Zulus wanted peace did nothing to diminish British determination. They had an invasionary force of nearly 18,000 men at the ready and by any estimate the assault on Zululand should not have been overtaxing. But two weeks in, reeling from the shock of Isandlwana, the British had to retreat to Natal and wait for reinforcements from England.

Over the years historians have laboured to explain how the mightiest of armies could have fallen. 'There were only sixty British survivors,' said Ian Knight, 'so the accounts of what happened are incredibly thin on the ground. It gave the military élite the perfect opportunity to write their own skewed account for the history books. They knew that Victorian society in 1879 could not countenance that the good old Brits fell foul of a bunch of black savages waving spears. So they tried – I think successfully – to pass the battle of Isandlwana off as an aberration.'

Although Knight is a historian, he has a personal reason for wanting to see the whole story re-examined. In 1998 he discovered that his own great-uncle, Thomas Cooper, was at Isandlwana. 'The papers turned up in a family attic. A relative of mine who knew I was interested in things military gave me a call one day and said look, I've got this stuff here, if you're interested Ian, come down and see what you think. And the first thing that I saw was a little memorial card saying that this chap had been killed actually at Rorke's Drift, and I couldn't believe it, what a strange coincidence.'

In fact, it turned out that Cooper was not killed at Rorke's Drift at all; he died at Isandlwana, a clear indication of the confusion in the public and – possibly – the military minds about the two battles.

Ian Knight's opportunity to get at the full truth of the massacre came when he accepted the position of adviser to a team of battlefield archaeologists who had been granted permission to examine the site. Chief Archaeologist and instigator of the project, Dr Tony Pollard, explained the approach their investigation would take. 'What we have to remember is that so few men survived this battle that the eyewitness accounts that are written down are very sparse and few and far between. If we view ourselves as forensic scientists looking at a crime scene – if you can call a battle a crime – and look at the physical remains, then through those remains and their distribution across the field we can start to tell the story from a different angle, from the angle of objects that have been dropped during the course of that battle.'

With the aid of metal detectors and cautiously handled digging tools, evidence of the British encampment was quickly uncovered. Among the first artefacts lined up for examination was a 7-pound artillery shell, a tent peg as big and heavy as a dagger, cavalry spurs, stirrups, insignia including the brass regimental number 24, and a piece of the lid of a pot bearing the words 'United Services Tooth Paste'. One truly remarkable find was a metal sovereign case which looked like an uncommonly thick silver locket; when it was opened there was a single gold sovereign inside, still bright and shiny, dated 1877.

What actually happened to the unsuspecting soldiers at their camp at Isandlwana Mountain is not disputed. Anxious to hunt down the Zulu army, Lord Chelmsford was enticed to leave his camp just after 3:30 a.m. on the morning of 22 January 1879. There had been reports of Zulus nearby and he smelt an opportunity to run down their army. Chelmsford's war party was made up of four guns of the Royal Artillery with about sixty men, six companies and the band of the 2nd and 24th Foot Regiment, 122 mounted troops, sixteen companies of the Natal Native Contingent totalling roughly 1,660 men, and ninety volunteer pioneers. In all, the force numbered approximately 2,500 officers and men, each man carrying one day's cooked rations and seventy rounds of ammunition. Lord Chelmsford and his staff rode ahead. 'Chelmsford left the camp without really making any preparations for its defence,' said Ian Knight. 'It was well known in the British high command that the thing to do really was either to entrench a camp or to form the wagons into a defensive circle, so that you've got some sort of permanent barricade that allows you to oppose any mass attack. The general feeling amongst the British, however, was that the Zulus would never actually have the nerve to mount the sort of attack that would get them close to a British camp. As a result, Chelmsford really underestimated what was necessary to defend the camp. He marched out, leaving an inadequate force to defend quite a wide area.'

And that was to be the main problem, a force sorely reduced in numbers trying to defend a camp area spread out over the best part of three-quarters of a mile, against what turned out to be a far more determined attack than they would have anticipated. As daylight dawned, Chelmsford and his troops were scattered across the hills, pursuing small bands of Zulus, trying to pin them down and bring them to battle. 'What's not happening while he's out here,' Ian Knight said, 'is that neither himself nor any of his staff are giving any thought to what might or might not be happening back at his camp.'

Erected as it was at the foot of Isandlwana Mountain, the camp was prominently sited. However, on the higher ground where Chelmsford and his men found themselves that hot morning, the mountain had dropped away out of sight. It was probable, too, that distance and the natural baffling effect of landmasses diminished any sound from the direction of the camp. The cries and screams and explosions of battle would not have been heard. Ian Knight tells a story of an officer who was with Chelmsford that day, who went up to a high point and looked back at the Isandlwana camp through his field glasses. He said that as he looked, he thought he saw a shadow pass across the foot of the mountain, then he glanced up and realized there were no clouds in the sky. In retrospect, we can only wonder if he had seen the Zulu army sweeping through the camp.

The Zulu decoys who had induced Chelmsford to mount up and leave camp, taking with him roughly half the available troops, had engineered a classic military strategy: they had divided their enemy. The way was clear for a Zulu force of 20,000 warriors to approach the undermanned camp at Isandlwana and take up the chest and horns formation devised by the mighty Shaka. As the 'chest' moved forward the 'horns' were already encircling the camp. The British were driven from their advance positions right back through the camp. By then the horns had almost closed in, cutting them off on either side. The remnants of the British force were then driven across rough terrain until they came to the bank of the Manzimnyama River, where the Zulus rounded them up and slaughtered them.

'There are some very graphic Zulu accounts of what the place was like after the battle was over,' said Ian Knight. 'In the immediate aftermath one warrior talks about the grass at the foot of Isandlwana being red with running blood, and the veldt [plain] was slippery, for it was covered with the brains and the entrails of the slain.'

Knight tells of an intriguing account by a Zulu boy who went to visit the battlefield a few days after the fighting was over. He had a talent for conveying what he saw and, simultaneously, what he felt. 'He said, "We saw dead things there. Dead was the horse, dead too the mule, dead was the dog, dead was the monkey, dead were the wagons, dead were the tents, dead were the boxes. Dead was everything, even to the very metals." He had this apocalyptic vision of an entire community, the whole British camp absolutely wiped out – men, horses, all the tents, all the equipment strewn around, scattered, everything appearing to be just completely destroyed.'

Specifically, the archaeological team were looking for clues that would explain the massacre in cold physical terms, in no way discoloured by emotion or prejudice. The battlefield is dotted across its length and breadth with cairns, pyramids of whitewashed stones, marking the communal graves of British soldiers where they fell. The progress of the fighting is discernible from the placement and number of the cairns. An aerial view shows the effectiveness of the Zulus' combined forward and pincer movement in herding the enemy together, killing them and cutting off those who retreated, eliminating the chance of escape except by a few. Dr Julie Roberts from Glasgow University is a forensic pathologist who worked with the archaeological team. She had already had experience of battlefield research in Kosovo, and it was her task at Isandlwana to attempt a determination of the causes of death from the remains buried under the cairns. She began at the stretch known as Fugitive's Trail, where the remaining soldiers were chased across rocky terrain towards the river.

As the stones were moved aside it became clear that the graves were badly eroded and had been looted by scavengers. The digging was cautious, inching downwards through the soil by tiny stages, layer by layer. When Julie Roberts finally uncovered a number of bones, they turned out to be animal, not human. From their relatively large size, and the size of teeth found nearby, they appeared to be horse remains.

This did not surprise Ian Knight. He had heard a particularly horrifying story and this grave's location seemed to fit the scenario. A gun carriage, pulled by four horses and led by several soldiers, chased by Zulus, fell down a precipice. The horses slid over the rocky edge above a ravine, but were held dangling by the jammed gun carriage behind them. As the horses hung there they were slashed to pieces by the Zulus; the same happened to the soldiers as they tried to scramble away.

As Julie Roberts probed further into the grave she found metal buckles and pieces of bridle leather, artillery buttons, and finally a human leg bone. This looked like fair confirmation that they had found the spot where the artillery met their end.

From the clustered groupings of many of the cairns, and the fragmentary remains in the upper stratum of the earth, a picture began to emerge: Isandlwana had not been a battle, but a rout. Men had been hacked down with extreme ferocity as they fled for their lives. It was decided that the second cairn to be opened should be the last one on Fugitive's Trail. If any human remains were found there, they could prove that British soldiers had been chased for nearly two miles over rocky ground and through thorn trees, before they were cut off by the river. As the dig progressed, Ian Knight became increasingly aware of the bloody reality of what happened to his own great-uncle. 'I've found it quite a moving experience to be involved in this dig,' he said. 'In lots of ways I have lived in the shadow of this mountain all of my working life, and it's been quite a strange experience, having a relative who was killed here. That's something which has haunted me when I've been writing about the battle, just that extra little nuance, and it's quite a strange experience now to be delving amongst the bones of men who were killed here, metaphorically looking on the face of my own dead relative who was here. I think certainly it has brought home the horror of this particular battle to me in a way that written accounts, even though you read them all the time when you're studying it, never quite do.'

The opening of the second cairn produced immediate and definite evidence of human remains. Julie Roberts identified a large bone fragment as occipital bone, from the back of the head. It was a thick bone, which probably explained why it survived so close to the surface. There was also a petrous temporal bone, from inside the skull, which contains the structures of the inner ear; this part of the skull's structure is remarkable for its hardness and density, and it can even survive cremation. 'These are useful for working out how many individuals you've got in a mass-grave situation,' Julie said, 'because they tend to survive so well.'

One of the most intriguing finds from the grave was a whole human tooth. 'It's a large molar, a maxillary molar – it's from the upper jaw – and it's in quite good condition. There's not a lot of wear in it, so it's not from an elderly adult, which we wouldn't expect, anyway.'

The rigorous standards of forensic archaeology being what they are, the team still could not be sure that a redcoat made it all the way to the far end of Fugitive's Trail. The remains may not have been British. Mingled in with the human bone were broken fragments of pottery which certainly were not British, they were Zulu. Julie Roberts pointed out that one fragment had been mistaken for a stone and had been whitewashed, but tribal patterning was clearly visible on the surface. 'We found up to forty fragments,' she said. 'There are probably two vessels there, and there is a tradition whereby a Zulu will come to a grave and smash pottery in honour of the ancestors.'

The degree of carnage which confronted the burial parties sent to Isandlwana six months after the massacre meant that mistakes were inevitable. A Zulu warrior may have been buried under the cairn in error, so to prove that British soldiers had been hunted down that far from the camp, the team would have to produce evidence that the bone fragments belonged to a redcoat. DNA testing was the only sure way.

The hundred-odd-year-old tooth was the best preserved piece of human material taken from the grave. In the laboratory tiny amounts of DNA were extracted from it; this was done by placing a powdered section of the specimen into a tube with a complex enzyme solution designed to separate DNA from a sample of human tissue. Once the powdered tooth had been added to the solution the tube was shaken thoroughly, then put into a water bath with a temperature of 60 degrees Celsius, a procedure designed to coax out any remaining DNA. Following that the tube was placed in a centrifuge, a high-speed rotating device used to separate the sample fragments from the solution. By that time, the solution would contain any DNA that might have resided in the sample. Next, making use of a chemical process known as a polymerase chain reaction (PCR), a large number of copies of the DNA were made in order to conduct as many tests as might be necessary to determine the genetic identity of the tooth.

African and European genetic codes are different. By comparing the extracted DNA with a control sample of European DNA, microbiologists and others can on most occasions obtain a coherent result, and in this case they did. A specialist explained that when they compared the two samples, they were identical. 'It would be very rare to find this DNA sequence in a sub-Saharan African, and there is strong evidence that it came from a British person as opposed to an African.' So the investigative team at Isandlwana could be reasonably sure that British soldiers had made it all the way to the end of Fugitive's Trail, to the point where it met the Manzimnyama River.

The team was also concerned about the confusing scale and ferocity of the massacre. It was inconceivable that an army as well equipped as the British should ever have found themselves in this position. The Zulus had 20,000 men, the British 1,600, so perhaps it was simply that they were outnumbered. But the British were armed with the Martini-Henry rifle, the most up-to-date and efficient weapon in its class at that time, or so the top brass believed. Martin Hinchcliffe, a weapons expert from the National Army Museum, said that the Martini-Henry .45, in ideal conditions, was probably the most effective weapon the British army had seen for many years. 'It was like having a modern fighter plane or tank.'

The weapon has an interesting history. In 1867 the Swiss government bought 15,000 Peabody rifles from the USA. After field-testing them for a few weeks, the Swiss military command felt that the weapons could be improved. They asked Friedrich von Martini, based in Lausanne, to do the job. Martini was a talented engineer rather than a gunsmith, but his knowledge of ballistics and firearms was wide ranging, and he was an accomplished firearms designer. He decided to alter the basic structure of the rifle, which was fitted with a breech-block hinged at the rear. This was operated by an under-lever and opened the breech by dropping down at the front, so that fresh cartridges could be slid into the chamber at the top of the block. An external hammer was cocked and then the breech was closed. When the trigger was pulled, the hammer struck a firing pin built into the breech-block.

Martini's first attempt at improvement involved altering the mechanism so that the hammer cocked automatically when the breech was opened. But he wasn't entirely happy with that. He finally eliminated the hammer and redesigned the firing pin inside the breech-block so that it cocked automatically as the breech was opened. Not only was this a much neater arrangement, it cut down the time between the trigger being pulled and the cartridge exploding; a period known as the 'lock time'. Martini's achievement was considerable, because it not only led to a smoother and faster action of fire-and-reload, it meant that the shorter the lock time, the less likely it was that the soldier's aim would drift, therefore the rifle's accuracy was effectively improved.

In 1867 the British Army was looking for a breech-loading replacement for the Snider conversion they had been using up to that time. They tested a number of weapons and finally settled on the Martini breech action described above; they combined the action with a barrel designed by a Scottish gunsmith, Alexander Henry. The British-built Martini-Henry .45 calibre rifle was finally introduced into service with the British Army in April 1871 and remained their standard weapon for many years. Surprisingly, a number of Martini-Henry .45 calibre rifles were still being used by local defence units in the area of the Suez Canal as recently as 1950.

The British soldiers at Isandlwana on the fateful day of 22 January 1879, could reload their weapons quickly and fire at a rate of about twelve rounds a minute, from an effective range of 800 feet. That day, each soldier would only have had to hit his mark six times and the Zulu force would have been cut to half. There has been speculation that some bullets may have been deflected by the Zulus' cow-hide shields. To test this, .45 calibre bullets from an original Martini-Henry rifle were fired at various distances and angles at shields of the exact kind used by the

Zulu Army in the late nineteenth century; in every case the bullets passed clean through. Bullets fired into blocks of specially compounded ballistic soap help the police to determine what gun has been used in cases of murder by showing what damage has been wrought; the blocks of soap are the same thickness as the human body and the same density as human flesh. Tests made with the soap and the Martini-Henry rifle showed that one well-aimed British bullet had enough velocity and penetrating power to kill more than one Zulu.

The power of the rifle could easily have compensated for the fact that the British were outnumbered at Isandlwana. There had to be other reasons for the scale of the defeat. One theory was that the ammunition ran out, but metal ring-pulls from the tops of the ammunition boxes were dug up from the battlefield, at positions not far behind the main firing line. 'The fact that we're finding definite evidence of ammunition boxes being opened on the line,' said Tony Pollard, 'suggests that they were being supplied as the battle was raging.' Men weren't having to run back to the supply wagons to get more boxes of bullets, they were being brought to them right on the firing line, so shortage of ammunition was no answer to the riddle of the massacre.

An almost desperate necessity to prove that something obstructed the troops from performing efficiently led some early commentators to suggest that screwdrivers, necessary to remove the single screw holding the boxes shut, were in short supply. But lots of screws from ammunition boxes were turning up on the battlefield dig, some of them bent curiously out of shape. An experiment revealed not only why they were bent, but also why the British soldiers never ran out of ammunition: in desperate circumstances, they found their own way of stocking up on bullets. 'The 24th was a very experienced regiment and would have been in action many times before,' said Ian Knight, 'using these rifles, using this ammunition, using this ammunition box. It's always seemed pretty inconceivable to me that they wouldn't know how to get into their own ammunition boxes. I think personally if I was there on the day I would find absolutely any means possible to get into the things. I think that nothing would stimulate the imagination more under these circumstances then twenty thousand warriors coming to kill you.'

The weapon of choice for the experiment, Knight explained, was the butt end of a Martini-Henry carbine, which he believed might have been something they used on the day at Isandlwana. The ammunition box was turned on its back and one end propped on a rock, the front of the box facing upwards. With a single blow of the gun butt, Ian Knight knocked the box lid free of its single retaining screw, simultaneously opening the box to expose the ring pull and, in the process, bending the screw. After such a swift, effortless manoeuvre, all a redcoat would have had to do was draw back the ring pull and uncover a fresh supply of ammunition.

So the slaughter of the British troops at Isandlwana in 1879 could not be explained by a lack of men, a lack of firepower, or a shortage of ammunition. There had to be something else. There were still some serious blanks for the archaeological team to fill in.

Experiments on the Martini-Henry rifle were still going ahead. In its day it was state-of-the-art weaponry, but there was always the possibility that on the day of the massacre, for whatever reason, it had let the riflemen down. One disadvantage, inherent in the ammunition, was that every time the rifle was fired, a cloud of dense white smoke obstructed the soldier's vision, and in calm weather the smoke took a long time to disperse. In a situation of rapid fire, it actually built up to form a smokescreen. Weapons expert Martin Hinchcliffe pointed out that when a soldier was peering through the tiny rear sight of the rifle, he never knew if he had hit his target until the smoke either cleared or thinned sufficiently to let him see. 'That's not too bad when you're a single shooter, but when you've got a thousand men shooting, you've got a dense white wall of smoke. Men could just appear through the smoke and be on top of you before you knew it.'

But on the afternoon of the battle, it wasn't just the smoke that reduced the visibility for the British soldiers. There was a solar eclipse. Martin Hinchcliffe found it easy to imagine, 'You're blasting away with walls of smoke in front of you and somebody switches the lights out. What can you see then? You're completely in the dark. Literally.'

Poor visibility could certainly have hampered the British that day, but again, as with so many other possible setbacks, it does not convincingly explain the monumental scale of the defeat. Perhaps, instead of trying to explain astonishing defeat on the field of battle, it would be more enlightening to investigate surprising success in the same setting. History has all but ignored the skills of the Zulu as a fighting force; the archaeological team were convinced that this was the direction to pursue in the search for a solution to the mystery. 'We're not, as archaeologists, saying that history is bunk,' said Tony Pollard, 'but it can be flawed and it can be biased. This battle for so long has been looked at as a British disaster, and an embarrassment, and "Why did they do so badly here?" But what we *really* need to start doing is look at why there was such a great Zulu victory here.'

Forty years of apartheid in South Africa blocked any exploration of a black victory, leaving the Zulus cast until now as a marauding horde of bloodthirsty savages. Tales of ritual mutilation performed on British soldiers lying dead on the battlefield effectively upheld the barbaric image. 'There are things which were done in Africa,' said Credo Mutwa, 'there are things which were done by my people, the Zulus, amongst many other people, which were seen by the white men, especially from England, as acts of barbaric savagery. And one of these things was that when a Zulu warrior had killed an English soldier, he used to come back, perhaps several hours later, to disembowel this enemy and others that he had brought down. Now, this disembowelling of English soldiers was used in Victorian England to arouse an intense anti-Zulu sentiment which has lasted until now. But, why did the Zulu people disembowel their enemies? It was not every enemy who qualified for disembowelment. Why? Because only enemies who had fought with honour were disembowelled afterwards. Only enemies who had proved chivalrous and brave qualified for this ancient ritual.'

Credo Mutwa went on to say that in order to understand another person, it is often wise to take a mirror and observe yourself. He pointed out that under an ancient Celtic tradition a respected enemy was decapitated and his head cleaned down to a skull, which was used as a drinking bowl by the warrior who had killed him. This was not an insult, Credo insisted, it was an act of respect towards an enemy. In ancient Japan, similarly, Samurai warriors who had fought with honour were decapitated by their enemies. The hair on the heads was dressed, and the heads were kept in a shrine by the man who had killed them.

'Our people believed and still believe in reincarnation,' Credo went on. 'We believe that when a man had just died violently and quickly, his soul gets trapped in his body, unable to go on into the great circle of rebirth. So, if this man is an honourable enemy, you must open his bowels, you must disembowel him in order to release his soul, so that it may go away to the next world.'

If the Zulus' high regard for the bravery of their enemy had been overlooked perhaps there was more besides that had been dismissed as merely primitive – their weapons, for example. 'The Zulus were reliant on close-quarter combat to win their battles,' said Ian Knight, 'and psychologically they embraced it. The whole Zulu fighting outlook was to get to grips with the enemy as quickly as possible and fight him at close quarters, to the extent that the word "stabbing", for example, was used as a metaphor for fighting. They were accustomed to using close-quarter weapons in their everyday lives, they grew up with spears and club sticks. They were extremely good, adept, skilled close-quarter fighters. Man-for-man they were probably better than the British at close-quarter combat.'

Using a traditional *knobkerrie* – a short thick stick with a knobbed head, which in this case was also faceted – Ian Knight demonstrated the power of close quarter combat by striking a cow's skull a single sharp blow. As a witness, Dr Julie Roberts was impressed. 'It's completely disrupted the skull and split it longitudinally in two, straight down the middle,' she said. 'In a living person the skin around the skull would have held it together to a certain extent, but there would still have been massive fracturing.'

Ian Knight then demonstrated the effectiveness of the other weapon commonly carried by Zulu warriors, the assegai. He brought the point down sharply on another animal skull; the sharp tip of the weapon penetrated the skull easily, emerging at the base. 'This is a typical example of sharp force trauma with a thin blade,' said Julie Roberts. She pointed to the clean thin slot at the point of entry, with fractures radiating off on either side. 'Pretty deadly'.

But it wasn't just the Zulus' weapons that made them such a formidable force on the battlefield. From the moment the commanders gathered their 20,000 warriors on the neutral ridge above the British camp, they displayed an eerie ability to act as a single fighting unit, with an uncommonly intense focus on their enemy. Prior to battle, the entire fighting unit chanted rhythmically, banging their shields and spears on the ground, building up the tempo, raising the volume until it reached a crescendo and the roar of impending carnage could be heard for miles. At a signal from their leaders they ran down the hillside and swept through the redcoats' camp, unstoppable, an intensely focused war machine tuned to kill.

The warriors' prodigious level of confidence preceded the chanting on the ridge, which was used to accelerate their already spectacular readiness for battle. Their confidence and concentration arose from ceremonies performed before they set off for the battle. 'They went through a whole series of rituals before they set off on a campaign, which effectively cut them off from everyday civilian life,' said Ian Knight. 'Once they had undergone these rituals their whole psychological intent was to go out and kill the enemy and they couldn't actually rejoin ordinary civilian society until they had done it. They lived in this universe of battle with everything focused upon the destruction of the invader, until they had actually gone out there and fought them, with the result that this was unleashed in a terrific frenzy of violence at the height of the battle itself.'

The effect of an elaborate series of chants, dances, and songs unified the warriors, giving them an intense singleness of purpose. 'You had to be bound together, friend to friend, group to group,' said Credo Mutwa. 'You had to act as one. People, when acting in a ritual, fused together and became one critical mass facing an enemy, it's as simple as that.'

The psychological effects of ritual in binding the Zulus together could have been only part of the secret of their ferocity in battle. At Isandlwana they smashed the power of the most sophisticated fighting force in the world, and they did it with apparent ease. This hinted at something more potent than single-mindedness.

'There are some strange descriptions which emerge from Zulu sources,' said Ian Knight, 'particularly when they are talking about the intense last moments of some of these battles, when the fighting was hand-to-hand. They picture themselves as being in a very intense state of mind, they say that they're seeing nothing but red, they're almost consumed with a type of blood lust, which gives a certain hallucinogenic quality to their accounts of the actual fighting.'

Time and again, Zulu warriors spoke of a veil of blood over their eyes. Other accounts were stranger still.

'They talk about seeing apes dressed in British uniforms, manning the British positions, and they seem to suggest that the British have been able to control nature and direct it against them because they say they saw strange birds coming to attack them from the British positions. One is left to ponder exactly what these accounts are referring to.'

A clue to the source of the hallucinatory episodes was perhaps to be found among the ingredients used in the Zulus' medicinal preparations, or *muti* as they were known. Credo Mutwa explained that medicine played an intensely important role in Zulu warfare. 'The war machine of the Zulu nation was backed up by a highly sophisticated medical corps,' he said, 'a corps of healers and traditional surgeons whose purpose was to heal all kinds of wounds that an army could sustain in battle.'

But there was more to war medicine than healing. Among other preparations that a warrior would carry with him, in a hollow horn strung around his neck, there was a potent snuff mixture. Again, Credo Mutwa explained. 'The snuffs that we used in the battle had the effect – whether actual or psychological, I don't know – they had the effect of concentrating your vision, making you very focused.'

Ian Knight acquired a quantity of the snuff and it was taken back to Britain for chemical analysis. Under the microscope the finely ground powder looked like cannabis, which has a very distinctive appearance. Powdered tobacco was present, too. A filtration test was run on the snuff: its make-up was confirmed as being a cannabis-tobacco mixture, though the highly unusual chemical composition of the cannabis indicated it was no ordinary variety. Cannabis contains a number of cannabinoids, which are its active constituents, the main ones being THC (tetrahydrocannabinol) and CBD (cannabidiol). THC is the psychoactive ingredient, in other words it makes people high although it can also cause anxiety and irritability, whereas CBD has a mellowing, rather sedative effect. In the sample of Zulu snuff, the major component was THC, and the chemists could find no trace of CBD. Such a high concentration of a psychoactive component, without the softening effects of CBD, would make a user abnormally alert. But what of the warriors' superhuman ferocity, the seeing red, and the hallucinations? Cannabis was not likely to account for that. Knowledge of the battle medicines used at Isandlwana was handed down from one generation to the next, and one medicine man who fought on that day told of a potion derived from a bulb. He passed on the secret to a young apprentice, his grandson Credo Mutwa, who revealed that the extract of the bulb had several names, one of them meaning 'the mirror'. 'This is a powerfully hallucinogenic bulb. It has the same effects as LSD, but it can be deadly when used carelessly. Today in Soweto, people use it to see into the future.'

The warriors who took the preparation made from the bulb were the élite. It would push them to risk their lives, if necessary, for the sake of victory. 'You got a group of your really special warriors, men without fear, and together these men had to share a ritual, a very, very deep ritual,' said Credo. 'They drank a tea made with this bulb as a sacrament, and they were able to see more or less how the war would progress, what the enemy would do, and whether victory or defeat would be theirs. You see we had commandos too, in olden days. We had special suicide warriors whose duty was to penetrate enemy lines, and to get behind the enemy. This is what happened at Isandlwana when a crack group of warriors went behind the English lines, and were able to attack the English from behind.'

The bulbs can still be found growing in the wilds of South Africa, and a botanist actually found them on sale in a city *muti* market tucked under a motorway flyover. He confirmed that the bulb is highly toxic, and that an infusion made from the same bulb had been used by the Kalahari bushmen to poison their arrows. Medicinally, its skin is used as a binding to disinfect wounds and to kill pain. If taken in a liquid the pulpy part of the bulb was extremely hallucinogenic. A specimen bulb from the market was taken to the laboratories of the London University School for Pharmacy. Straightforward chemical analysis revealed that it was full of alkaloids. 'Morphine is an alkaloid,' explained a pharmacist, 'strychnine's an alkaloid, nicotine's an alkaloid. The major hallucinogens are all alkaloids. They're often very toxic.' Referring to the test results on the bulb, she said, 'These particular alkaloids do have a stimulating effect on the central nervous system, and they also have a painkilling effect rather like codeine or morphine. It would have two advantages, really, because you would have the stimulating effect – the alertness and the wakefulness – and you would have the painkilling effect, which would probably come in useful.'

As Credo Mutwa implied, this bulb could have been used by Zulu suicide squads. The pharmacist pointed out that the cocktail of alkaloids was too toxic for frequent use, but to a man in furious battle the long-term toxic effects were probably not an issue. It was clear by now that the use of medicines in warfare had become something of a high art among the Zulus.

There was one substance more powerful yet to be investigated. It was a hallucinogenic mushroom, once again used as a snuff. 'This mushroom snuff was only used by warriors who intended not to return alive from the battlefield,' said Credo. Tests carried out by a toxicologist determined that the main active ingredient of the mushroom in question is a substance which produces extraordinary mental detachment, and can eliminate anxiety or fear. 'Let us say that you wanted to kill as many of the enemy as possible before they killed you,' said Credo. 'You took this snuff, and the snuff would have a strange effect upon you. It would make you very, very thirsty, so you had to have a quantity of water close by to you. Then the snuff would also have the effect of making your eyes sort of glazed, like a person already dying. And the enemy coming towards you will think that you are already dying, looking at your eyes. But you are very, very alert, lost in a world of glorious illusion. And you will stand up and stab the enemy, two or three of them before you fall.'

Under the supervision of expert toxicologist Professor John Henry, from St Mary's Hospital in London, and a team of medics and psychologists, the mysterious red mushroom was tested on two evenly matched judo players, Christian and Craig. Judo was chosen as it is a modern form of combat that requires similar levels of focus and adrenalin as might be possessed by a warrior. The subjects had several bouts to set physiological and psychological base levels and then the mushroom was given to Christian; Craig was given a placebo. Within minutes the two fought again, but this time Christian flew at Craig, knocking him down with hitherto unseen strength. Talking to Professor Henry after the bout, Christian declared himself more focused and able to fight than he had ever felt before.

It was clear by now that the forces opposing the British Army at Isandlwana were awesome in the extreme, but even so, the British firing line should have withstood the onslaught far better than it did – no amount of Zulu bravery could stop bullets. Establishing how they broke through the line would mean locating hard forensic evidence of the British defensive position – specifically, a long line of spent cartridges.

The search began and archaeologist Tony Pollard explained what their findings told them. 'As the battle line breaks up, men are falling back into the camp, and the way we can pick up on that archaeologically is to find their footsteps, if you like, through the form taken by the cartridge cases they're dropping. At one point we made quite an exciting discovery. We found three Martini-Henry cartridge cases in a line behind one another, with about ten or twelve feet between them. Some distance in front of them we actually found a lead bullet. By the time that bullet was fired, probably from one of these cartridge cases we found in a row, the enemy were feet away from this guy, who's backing up, backing up, backing up. Those last three shots may well be the last three he fired before he was overrun.'

The history books have always said the British firing line extended 650 feet out from the camp from north to south, but the forensic team's digging and diligent sifting convinced them the line extended much further than that. The search took them a further 330 feet out beyond the fences of the battlefield reserve. 'And lo and behold,' said Tony Pollard, 'within ten minutes we found our first Martini bullet this side of the fence. Now one bullet obviously does not a firing line make, but the fact that we've got a single bullet beyond the fence means that the firing line is somewhere out here, because you wouldn't get a single bullet in front of the firing line.'

The single bullet is a crucial find. If the British extended their defence so far from the camp, it meant that each of the men had to defend a wider area. To do that, they would have had to break with their training to fire in formation, and spread themselves out several yards apart. 'Logic would suggest that's a very vulnerable and exposed position,' said Ian Knight. 'Despite the fact that there were probably three or four yards between each man in order to be able to cover that whole stretch of ground, they were completely confident that the firepower they could put down would be sufficient to stop the Zulus. Of course it didn't work out quite like that.'

A clear picture of how the British line was broken was beginning to emerge. 'It's very obvious,' said Tony Pollard, 'that once that firing line was broken, the battle was over quickly. These men were moving back very fast, they weren't firing that much ammunition because they didn't have the damn time to fire it. They weren't standing shoulder to shoulder, there was yards between them, and as soon as that thin red line was broken – to use the old cliché –the game was a bogey.'

The fact that the British soldiers were spread too wide apart could have been the central cause of their downfall; it was certainly a huge tactical mistake. If undue pressure was put on one man in an over-extended firing line, he would at once become a weak link in an already flimsy chain, a link that would soon give way and let the Zulus rush through.

But there was another factor for the investigative team to consider. Accounts from other battles that year mentioned the Martini-Henry rifle could, on occasion, jam when it was being reloaded. Under ideal conditions the weapon performed well, but the British at Isandlwana were not firing their rifles under ideal conditions. Each soldier was yards from the next man on either side, and was forced to discharge more rounds than he would if they were closer together.

Martin Hinchcliffe explained what was likely to happen. 'When the black powder burns it leaves a residue in the barrel. The drier and hotter it is, the harder this residue becomes, until you end up with a coating inside the barrel, like icing on a cake. So all these highly machined precision fits get fouled up solid by this cake of black powder.'

It is also a fact that Martini-Henry bullets were easily damaged. Hinchcliffe showed several whose cases had been dented and otherwise distorted simply by handling and dropping. The seconds wasted by one gun jamming could mean the end for everyone on a stretched-out firing line.

The team decided that tests should be carried out on a Martini-Henry rifle to see if repeated firing could cause the gun to jam. On the firing range, Martin Hinchcliffe took the temperature of the rifle barrel before testing began, and found, unsurprisingly, that it was at room temperature. The gun was then fired twelve times in quick succession, and the temperature of the barrel began to soar. After a total of twenty-four shots had been fired, the gun jammed. Repeat testing made it clear that several guns probably jammed in the heat of battle at Isandlwana.

The weapon's shortcoming was one more piece from a long-lost jigsaw. There are still many pieces to be located before the picture is entirely clear, but what has been found so far is compelling. On 22 January 1879, the formidable British force facing the oncoming Zulus at Isandlwana had just too much stacked up against them. They were so arrogantly sure of their superiority in battle that they stretched their red line suicidally thin. They underestimated the intelligence, skill, bravery, and commitment of their enemy. Even nature took a hand by adding an eclipse to the fog of gunsmoke, making the soldiers' white helmets and red tunics the only bright targets on the darkened field of battle. But, perhaps most lamentably of all, their prized weaponry simply was not up to the demands of battle against the Zulus.

As time passes much more may be discovered about the massacre at Isandlwana; perhaps, too, the same day's fighting at Rorke's Drift will take its due place in the history of minor skirmishes of the Zulu wars. Further investigation at the battlefield, whether it uncovers more important evidence or not, can do no harm. At best, it will set straight a record which for too many years has remained distorted.

BIBLIOGRAPHY

THE JAMESTOWN MASSACRE

History of the Virginia Company of London by E.D. Neill; B. Franklin (US), 1968

Jamestown Archaeology (various contributors); US Department of the Interior, 1985

Poisons and Toxins by Mark Kusinitz; Chelsea House Publishers (US), 1992

The Complete Works of Captain John Smith (1580–1631); 3 vols, University of North Carolina Press (US), 1986

The Pilgrims and Pocohontas by Ann Uhry Abrams; Westview Press (US), 1999

The Virginia Adventure by Ivor Noël Hume; University Press of Virginia (US), 1997

BLOOD ON THE ALTAR

Bones: Ancient Men and Modern Myths by Lewis R. Binford; Academic Press, 1981

Carthage, or the Empire of Africa by A.J. Church; T.F. Unwin, 1980

Phoenicians by Glenn E. Markoe; British Museum Press, 2000

The Highest Altar by Patrick Tierney; Viking, 1989.

The Interpretation of Ritual edited by J.S. La Fontaine; Tavistock Publications, 1972

The Phoenicians and the West by Maria Eugenia Aubet; Cambridge University Press, 1993

MURDER AT STONEHENGE

Forensic Osteological Analysis
edited by S.I. Fairgrieve; Charles
C. Thomas, 1999

*From Stonehenge to Modern
Cosmology* by Sir Fred Hoyle;
W. H. Freeman (US), 1972.

*Great Stone Circles: Fable, Fiction,
Facts* by Aubrey Burl; Yale
University Press (US), 1999

Relic, Icon, or Hoax? by
H.E. Gove; Institute of Physics
Publications, 1996

The Making of Stonehenge by
Rodney Castleden; Routledge,
1993

The Sphinx and the Megaliths by
John Ivimy; Turnstone, 1974

THE RIDDLE OF THE PLAGUE SURVIVORS

AIDS Sourcebook edited by Karen
Bellenir; Omnigraphics, 1999.

Antivirals against AIDS (various
contributors); Marcel Dekker
(US), 2000

Eyam Plague by John Clifford;
J.Clifford, 1995.

More Cunning than Man by
Robert Hendrickson; Stein and
Day, (US) 1983

Plague Manual by M. Bahmanyar
& D. C. Cavanaugh; World
Health Organization, 1976

The Great Plague by Stephen
Porter; Alan Sutton Publishing,
1999

THE REAL ZULU DAWN

Great Zulu Battles 1838–1906 by
Ian Knight; Cassell Military,
2000

Shaka Zulu by E.A.Ritter;
Greenhill Books, 1990

Shaka's Children by Stephen
Taylor; Ramboro Books, 1999

The Age of Empire by
E.J. Hobsbawm; Abacus, 1994

The Martini-Henry 1869–1900 by
B.A.Temple & I.D.Skennerton;
B.A. Temple, 1996

*The Rise and Fall of the Zulu
Nation* by John Laband; Cassell
Military, 1997

INDEX

plague 111–44
  attack on the immune
    system 133
  disappearance 132
  Great Plague of
    London 116–17
  immunity 132, 144
  isolation hospitals 112
  measures against
    111–12, 131
  scapegoating 133, 139
  survivors 117–18, 124
  treatments 131
  see also AIDS;
    bubonic plague
Plant, Joan 122–3, 127
Planton, Dennis 23, 24,
  25, 27
Pliny the Elder 56
Plymouth,
  Massachusetts 7
Pocahontas 15
Point Comfort 25
poisonings and
  poisoning plots
  against Elizabeth I 39
  Jamestown 29–36,
    39–41
  Native Americans 33
  see also arsenic
Pollard, Dr Tony 159,
  169, 171–2, 180–1
Polybius 49, 53, 54, 55
polymerase chain
  reaction (PCR) 72–3,
  166
Port Natal (Durban)
  149–50
Powhatan 15
Price, Hugh 30
Protestant English
  church 36
Punic Wars 49

racial inferiority thesis
  145, 146, 147
radio-carbon dating 85,
  89–90, 92, 93,
  100–1
Raleigh, Sir Walter 9

Ramsey, Dr
  Christopher 89–90, 101
rats 23, 118
ratsbane (arsenic) 33
reincarnation 173
Reynolds, Dr Andrew
  103, 104, 105, 106–7
Richards, Robin 107–8
ritual mutilation 172
RNA (ribonucleic acid)
  136, 137
Roanoke Island 9
Roberts, Dr Charlotte
  60–1, 62–3, 64
Roberts, Dr Julie 163,
  164, 165, 173–4, 174
Roman Britain 85–6,
  89, 93
Romans 42, 49, 52, 56,
  60
Rorke's Drift 155–6,
  158, 183
Royal College of
  Surgeons (RCS) 82

sacred prostitution
  100–1
sanitation 26–7, 48
sarsen 77, 78
Semple, Sarah 103
Senzangakona 147
Servadio, Gaia 54, 55
Shaka 147, 148, 149,
  150
Sicily 54, 55
Siculus, Diodorus 53
Sidon 43, 44
Siena 115
Sim, Dr David 94–7,
  98, 99–100
skeletons
  carbon dating 85,
    89–90, 92, 93,
    100–1
  child skeletons 61
  dental evidence 62–3,
    64–6, 90, 91–2,
    104–5, 165–6
  examining 19–21,
    61–2, 83–4

sex and age,
  determining 20,
    60–1, 68
skull and facial
  reconstruction
    20–1, 107–9
skin exfoliation 29, 32
Smith, Captain John
  12, 13, 14, 15, 16,
    29, 31, 33
Smith, Professor
  Patricia 65–6, 74
Smithsonian Institution
  20
snuff 176–7, 179
soil analysis 90–1
Stager, Professor Larry
  52–3, 57–9, 62, 67, 74
Stanley, John 39
stillborn children 58,
  64, 66
Stonehenge 76–110
  astronomical
    computer theory 80
  Aubrey Holes 77
  Avenue 78, 79
  construction 76, 77–9
  Druidic theory 80–1
  Heel Stone 77, 78, 80
  purpose and
    significance 79–81,
    103
  site description 76–7
  skeleton (4–10–4)
    81–5, 87, 88, 89,
    90–1, 91, 92–3, 95,
    97–100, 103, 105,
    106, 107–10
  Slaughter Stone 77
  Stonehenge I 76, 77, 78
  Stonehenge II 76, 78
  Stonehenge III 76,
    78, 79
  sun worship theory 80
Straube, Beverly 14, 23,
  37
Stringer, Professor
  Chris 92
strontium 19, 105–6
strychnine 178

PICTURE CREDITS